MEDICAL HUMANITIES AND DISABILITY STUDIES

IN/DISCIPLINES

Critical Interventions in the Medical and Health Humanities

Series Editors
Stuart Murray, Corinne Saunders, Sowon Park and Angela Woods

Critical Interventions in the Medical and Health Humanities promotes a broad range of scholarly work across the Medical and Health Humanities, including both larger-scale intellectual projects and argument-led provocations, to present new field-defining, interdisciplinary research into health and human experience.

Titles in the series
Abortion Ecologies in Southern African Fiction, Caitlin E. Stobie
Relating Suicide, Anne Whitehead
Covid-19 and Shame, Fred Cooper, Arthur Rose and Luna Dolezal

Forthcoming titles
Autism and the Empathy Epidemic, Janet Harbold
Reproductive Health, Literature, and Print Culture, 1650–1800, Ashleigh Blackwood

MEDICAL HUMANITIES AND DISABILITY STUDIES

IN/DISCIPLINES

Stuart Murray

BLOOMSBURY ACADEMIC
LONDON • NEW YORK • OXFORD • NEW DELHI • SYDNEY

BLOOMSBURY ACADEMIC
Bloomsbury Publishing Plc
50 Bedford Square, London, WC1B 3DP, UK
1385 Broadway, New York, NY 10018, USA
29 Earlsfort Terrace, Dublin 2, Ireland

BLOOMSBURY, BLOOMSBURY ACADEMIC and the Diana logo are trademarks
of Bloomsbury Publishing Plc

First published in Great Britain 2023

Cover design: Rebecca Heselton

A catalogue record for this book is available from the British Library.

A catalog record for this book is available from the Library of Congress.

ISBN: HB: 978-1-3501-7218-0
        PB: 978-1-3501-7217-3
        ePDF: 978-1-3501-7216-6 .
        eBook: 978-1-3501-7219-7

Series: Critical Interventions in the Medical and Health Humanities

Typeset by RefineCatch Ltd, Bungay, Suffolk
Printed and bound in Great Britain

To find out more about our authors and books, visit www.bloomsbury.com
and sign up for our newsletters.

In memory of my sister, Alison

CONTENTS

Provocation (Medicine): testing to elicit a particular response or reflex

OED

UNDIAGNOSED

'how every line was really a curve uncreased'

Lauren Slater

Was a black-bag boy with visions,
A low-tech mole who flicked,
Stood on corners, selling,
And said he had never seen the sea.
His days were cut from free school lunches
And no-show pickups,
Trimmed by pointless hours in the park.
Cold airless nights of misplaced words
With sleep always elsewhere, shadows estranged,
And each season a search for imagined atrocities.

Hyper, he grew to fidget and hustle visitors,
Made fake maps to show where they could get one more –
Pointing the way with a bonhomie just this side of panic.
Weather for evangelicals worked in his favour,
That and people's trust to believe in what they don't know,
Working backwards to the subject they hoped they could be.
He provided all this, with nothing more than a light smile
And a backstory of ingratiation.
He was sure he had learned something.

In middle age, released, he lost his way.
Confronted by people who made more sense than he did
He missed understanding: how could you come back
To precisely where you started?

And so, foxed and stuck in light,
He remained in rooms that reflected back the moment he left them,
Where soft walls promised correction, but preparations were insecure

Undiagnosed

And threatened violence.
He was where he had been,
Across the blank looks of those he had known,
Washed in their desire to be elsewhere:
An inheritance that was never his to begin with.

He was last seen where the road bent away,
The sky stitched in a dun orange,
And birds gathered.
I think he would want to tell you this if he could.

INTRODUCTION: MISSING WORDS, OR NOT OTHERWISE SPECIFIED

Not there

In the summer of 2019 I completed an academic monograph entitled *Disability and the Posthuman*, which is the longest book I have ever written. It is on the intersection of disability and posthumanism and looks especially at questions of bodies and technology in a range of mainly contemporary fictional texts. The project developed organically from previous research I've undertaken around disability and, speaking broadly, 'the human', particularly in relation to autism, and included newer interests in the relations between literary/cultural studies, engineering and robotics, and disability/health. I've worked in what is sometimes termed Critical or Cultural Disability Studies for nearly twenty years, looking at the representation and depiction of disability in fiction and film, and this latest book is very much a study driven by reading and interacting with scholarship in the field. At the same time, I have identified as a scholar who works in the broad area of Medical Humanities and been a director of a research centre focused on the discipline for ten years, discussing the critical paradigms, theories and methodologies provided by Medical Humanities that enable work on topics such as disability and health representations. I am probably as much of a Disability Studies/ Medical Humanities scholar as is possible and am very happy to be so. And yet, for all this positioning between the two disciplines and my commitment to both, the term 'Medical Humanities' does not occur once in *Disability and the Posthuman*; not as a theoretical framing or critical context, not as an enabling tool for textual analysis, not even in a footnote.

It is not that the contents and arguments of the book do not fit within what are understood to be the parameters of Medical Humanities. Its focus on disability and the body and on theories of technology, as well as its championing of cross-disciplinary critical methodologies, are squarely part of current research in the disciplines that address such topics, sometimes at length, and I have gained much from the thinking and writing that has developed to shape Medical Humanities as a discipline, especially in the UK, across the last ten years. My work now wouldn't be possible without this. Yet clearly I didn't think – and want to stress that this wasn't any conscious decision – that it was a necessary frame to mention explicitly in the book. It's a missing term, then, present as an invisible thread: there but not.

This isn't necessarily surprising; scholarship does this all the time. Writers trained during the height of poststructuralism (of which I'm one) don't feel the need to cite Derrida, Foucault or Kristeva in everything they produce; anyone whose ideas were formed by Geertz's deep play, Bourdieu's symbolic capital, or Barad's new materialism won't always devote the first paragraph of an article signposting how this heritage is vital to the writing that follows. Sometime a sentence does the job, or a footnote, or – usually the more you write and the further away you get from your first theoretical loves – the presence recedes as ideas become habitual and new structures of thought emerge. Equally, there's a temptation to say that Medical Humanities was missing because in fact it isn't important to use it in ways that might be necessary in a critical monograph. Like other names of disciplines or subject areas (Renaissance Studies, Gender Studies, Social and Public Policy), it could be argued that it's sort of *always* there and what matters is the details that come under the heading; that's where the work is done. In part this is true: any organizing label is to some degree a convenience (this is of course true of Disability Studies as well, a term I use a lot in the posthumanism book) but it also strikes me as an evasion, at least in part. In my experience, the main reason for this is benign: scholars sometimes simply don't feel that a particular heading describes what they do, or they believe that another term does the job better. Arguably, most people working in Disability Studies ignore work undertaken in Medical Humanities, often for these reasons though equally at times because of suspicions about its methods. Why change the habits of a lifetime?

But I didn't want to evade Medical Humanities when writing my last book, and the thinking it has enabled is there in the prose. In addition, I'd argue that the organizational element of any discipline or critical model is in fact foundational to the scope and scale of its arguments. To view a discipline's title as only an umbrella term is to miss its status as a critical concept that itself produces work through establishing parameters, and you can always see a little more clearly how people think by looking at the boundaries of that thinking, what gets included and what is felt to be beyond legitimate enquiry. Possibly Medical Humanities is different to examples of older academic disciplines because of its novelty and evolving status in a fast-developing contemporary critical landscape. For those of us working in the area, it is maybe less the formative nature of what we have read and more the active inspiration of what we are reading that counts. But in my case the words *are* missing and it's maybe productive to stop thinking around the issue and ask if there is anything to be learned by concentrating on the absence.

Both Medical Humanities and Disability Studies contain their fair share of missing and absences. As with any body of scholarship, the disciplines shape-shift; ideas and priorities come and go, and heritages are contested and left behind, but still linger. For some researchers, vital topics are underexplored or not even covered at all, while others disagree about critical directions and vocabularies. A book such as this one needs to map, as much is possible, what each term means, where it comes from and how it works, and what it might do in the future. But undertaking this involves an acknowledgement of an inherent slipperiness in the process, a recognition of ignorance and, at times, avoidance. Both disciplines deal with the grounded lives of people and the structures that surround these, but both are also highly theorized with input from numerous subject areas.[1] Each has a home within the academy but also a commitment to reach beyond academic institutions and modes of thought. With all that ambition, it's not surprising that things go missing.

Essential to this is to view and understand both Medical Humanities and Disability Studies as *systems*. They are networks of communication and assemblages of critical thought. It is in seeing their organizations and workings – their various interfaces, methodologies, communities and outlets – as being systemic *effects* that we are better able to understand their aims and contribution to knowledge. For the purposes of making this book work, I will sometimes use the somewhat clunky practice of characterizing them, saying for example that 'Disability Studies works towards …' or a similar phrase. What I mean when I say this is that 'the fluid and cluttered processes of Disability Studies as a system work towards …'. My shorthand is to provide clarity, not to simplify or reify the subject. It is interesting that Medical Humanities is still sometimes referred to through the definite article ('*the* Medical Humanities') in a process that seems to hold it up as a particular distinct identity, the discipline *as discipline*. In fact this can be turned on its head, with the peculiar focus being seen as an invitation to unpick the systems that accrue to make it 'the'. What gets hidden and goes missing in making Medical Humanities seemingly so distinct? This is a far more interesting question than its (often powerful) presence as a badge.

I also want to claim that there are specific and important details attached to missing words when it comes to thinking about medicine and health.

When we experience ill health or have a disability, we often want to find the word that names how we feel, what the pain means, or the condition we have, the future we might expect. Equally it helps to know a term we might ascribe to others, so that we are less embarrassed or unsure when we engage with them or talk about them. It is a learning experience of some complexity when we realize that often this word doesn't exist, that our health and that of others might be suspended between words, or that the word we are given can turn out to be wrong. Diagnosis and prognosis are moments that are full of words. They might be comforting, terrifying or mystifying, they might need Google to explain and unpack them, but they are rarely without meaning. At times, they cover up the words that are not used and could be more explanatory and enabling. What's there and what's missing take on important shapes. Health becomes absence as much as presence.

Specifications

'Not otherwise specified' (NOS) is a term found in medical texts such as the *Diagnostic and Statistical Manual of Mental Disorders* (*DSM*) and *International Classification of Diseases* (*ICD*) that is used to describe behavioural, neurological and mental health conditions. In the most recent edition of *DSM* – *DSM V* – it has changed to 'Not Elsewhere Classified', an interesting migration between specifying and classifying, and contexts ('otherwise' and 'elsewhere'), but its presence works in the same way. It is a subcategory that usually comes at the end of sections in which the symptoms of various conditions, often vital for diagnosis, are outlined and listed, and is designed to catch manifestations of ill health not covered by the manuals' previous specific diagnostic criteria. NOS can itself at times be divided, between 'other specified' and 'unspecified' formations for example, and is intended to work by giving clinicians the greatest possible flexibility to capture accurately the features with which a patient might present ('capture' is an important word here, oscillating as it does between ideas of accuracy and entrapment).

One of the most used examples of NOS has been in relation to Personality Disorders (PDs). PDNOS was introduced in the fourth edition of the DSM in 1994, specifically as a category to be used when a patient's symptoms did not fall into any one of the existing ten defined PDs. As such, the assumption was that it would be used rarely, and it does not have the criterion-based or diagnostic detail that are central to other PDs. Unexpectedly, it has come to be one of the most commonly diagnosed PDs: around 20 per cent of PD diagnoses are NOS and research notes that in some diagnostic interview situations, it is often the most frequently used. This outcome appears less about its status as a category and more the complexity of, and lack of consensus around, trying to define a personality disorder. PDNOS brings together what seems to be a set of incompatible elements: its diagnostic status is secure, yet it has an absence of symptoms; and although it is increasing as a diagnosis, its existence as a subcategory means that those diagnoses are difficult to validate because of their shifting position in the context of PDs more generally.[2] PDs themselves seems to promote dissatisfaction: one 2007 study called the domain 'arbitrary, often unreliable, overlapping, and incomplete', with only a 'limited utility for treatment planning' and noted that 'the assessment of personality disorder is currently inaccurate, largely unreliable, frequently wrong, and in need of improvement'. At the same time, another investigation in the same year argued that it is precisely this unreliable and inaccurate incompleteness that provides possibilities for greater clarity, offering an opportunity for 'the field [to] work toward a single, hierarchical, integrated framework' that has the 'the potential to revolutionize our entire field'.[3] Add 'Not Otherwise Specified' to this as a largely detail-free sub layer and you have a potential storm of nothing and everything.

Possibly it helps to think of 'Not Otherwise Specified' in terms of words. The term is three words used when other words can't name fully the detail evidenced in the health of the person being diagnosed. It puts something unspecified in a specified place. It is a reminder of Virginia Woolf's observation, in her 1926 essay 'On Being Ill', of how it is precisely 'the poverty of the language' surrounding health that causes so many problems when trying to express its effects. 'English', she writes, 'which can express the thoughts of Hamlet and the tragedy of Lear, has no words for the shiver and the headache [...] let a sufferer try to describe a pain in his head to a doctor and the language at once runs dry'. Woolf's point is not that the pain of ill health makes language impossible, as some theorists have argued, rather that it places words under pressure and creates a need for innovation, a language 'more primitive, more sensual, more obscene', as she puts it; words more attuned to the materiality of embodiment.[4] Woolf's call is for language about illness to be fit for purpose, and for all that it appeared nearly 100 years ago, her essay mirrors the idea of the troubled clinical space in which NOS tries to work, a place of words used when other words miss their target. The spaces of the *DSM* and *ICD*, we might also add, are environments where words are especially important, given that they carry the added responsibility of the use value inherent within diagnosis and the power this value can wield.

The idea of *specification* raises questions about the efficacy of words as they relate to both medicine and disability. Most associated with psychiatry and mental health, NOS is also a term used in the manuals for diagnoses of cognitive disabilities and specific neurobehavioral conditions; its problematic configuration of words, what they can and can't do, opens a door on to a consideration of disability more widely. Autism was one condition in the *DSM* with the NOS label, a category I remember wrestling with for some time. I have worked on, and lived with, autism for twenty years, and have watched the meaning of the word change. Increasingly I feel that it seems to have become one stretched to breaking point, becoming a spectrum (not only clinical, but also linguistic) potentially so poorly articulated that its specificity appears to have vanished. Often, I struggle to see exactly where the word autism is now located, or to understand what it includes, what it *specifies*. It has considerable impact within Disability Studies, functioning as a site of identification and collective belonging, a presence that can be far-reaching. For example, experience-led advocacy helped the UK Parliament pass the 2009 Autism Act, which requires the State to provide service provision for adults with autism, structured through legally binding guidance given to local authorities. More widely, the condition, as Joseph Straus has noted, is a culture, with a vision, coherence and set of meanings – a 'distinctive cognitive style and worldview' – that articulate processes of claim and an assertion of rights.[5] It has driven a greater recognition of neurodiversity that now operates in many public discourses. At times, however, it functions in classic NOS mode, like a catch-all term for cognitive difference, a state of mind and set of behaviours with unidentifiable characteristics because it can include so much variation. Not only does it lack specificity, it sometimes appears that it can become what anyone (whether individuals or collectives) want it to be.

When autism the word frustrates me in this way, when I feel that it has become normalized to a point where specifics almost seem not to matter, I try to re-centre myself by looking at the *work* it does. The power of association and claim is often palpable for people that have been cast out and undervalued: witness the relief and satisfaction that often comes with an adult diagnosis ('*now* I know why I have always felt that way'). These kinds of achievements cannot be overestimated given how recently this kind of identification was impossible; in the past, autism has been made a freakshow and a site of injustice, so for it now to carry the banner of pride is wonderful. At the same time, the word's proliferation has led to a different kind of abuse. Take the case of Alek Minassian, who drove a van into a crowd in Toronto in April 2018, killing ten people in an act of incel-motivated murder that also injured sixteen others. Minassian admitted planning and carrying out the attack, but pleaded not guilty to murder, a plea his defence counsel expanded by claiming that his autism prevented him from making rational choices and understanding the moral consequences of his actions. Giving detail to this, his legal team argued that he lacked the capacity to 'understand fully why it is morally wrong to kill people' because he saw them as simply 'objects'.[6] A March 2021 guilty verdict consigned that argument to the place it belongs, but it is worth noting that it is an example of another specification of autism, another way the word is made to work that carries the full heritage of the condition understood as somehow nonhuman. The legal arguments in the Minassian case are a reminder of how the increased recognition of autism allows for its abuse. One way or another, there is surely something of Woolf's language poverty – something unspecified – here.

In medicine, words come and go, move around, and elicit different responses. My original form of epilepsy when I was diagnosed in the 1980s was typified by what were termed grand mal fits, but now expresses itself under the heading of generalized tonic-clonic seizures, which is maybe more literal but lacks what I always thought of as the mystery and glamour of the French, even if those two words never translated to the actuality of experience. Most epilepsy doesn't take the form of Dostoevsky's 'ecstatic experience', though, and his character Prince Myshkin (the 'holy fool' in *The Idiots*) isn't really a model for understanding what a seizure is like, no matter what those of us who are drawn to literature to explain the world might want to argue. In her memoir *An Unquiet Mind*, psychiatrist Kay Redfield Jamison talks of her preference for the term 'manic-depressive illness' over 'bipolar disorder', noting that although her official diagnosis is the latter and that bipolar is 'now firmly entrenched in the nomenclature' of psychiatry, she finds it 'strangely and powerfully offensive: it seems to me to obscure and minimize the illness it is supposed to represent'. By way of contrast, Jamison observes, manic depressive 'seems to capture both the nature and the seriousness of the disease I have, rather than attempting to paper over the reality of the condition'. She adds that 'patients who have suffered from the illness should have the right to choose whichever term they feel more comfortable with', possibly an unusual attitude to naming rights from a clinician. It's clear, however, that words matter a lot when they come to be interwoven through a life.[7]

In her 1998 book *Claiming Disability*, Simi Linton has a characteristically sharp few pages in which she discusses the 'Nice Words' and 'Nasty Words' used to describe disability. The former include physically challenged, the abled disabled, handicapable and special people/children (it's worth remembering that these stem from discussions now twenty-five years old), while the latter are the more expected: cripple, vegetable, dumb, deformed, retard and gimp. But, Linton reminds us, the seemingly obvious distinction is not what it seems. When used within disability communities, cripple, freak and gimp have what she terms 'transgressive potential' and have become what we now recognize as important identity-first positions. She also recounts the story of encountering a section in a bookstore entitled 'Children with Special Needs' that had a separate bottom shelf with the label 'Misc. Challenges' for those books that don't fit standard – presumed positive – modes of 'challenge'.[8] In both these examples, words seem characterized as much by their potential mobility as by any ability to offer precise naming. Misc. Challenges certainly has a strong sense of NOS about it.

The words of medicine and disability evolve like the tech upgrades that, in fact, they often are. Drug labels and treatment terms move on. Some – Thalidomide, for example – remain in the lexicon as reminders of spectacular failure and harm. Others that have saved and transformed the lives of millions go by trade names that a majority of the population wouldn't recognize. The same impetus of change is true of academic disciplines. Disability Studies was once predominantly the province of sociological forms of enquiry, with a working model that fundamentally transformed an understanding of disability, especially in identifying processes of discrimination, and helped change lives in a manner that few academic concepts can ever hope to. As it first emerged in the US, Medical Humanities was a vehicle for bringing humanism and the power of the Arts to the training of clinicians. Both subjects have experienced their respective critical 'turns' that have seen them expand, in many ways radically, from their origins. They have changed and, in some cases, fractured, and what is evolution for one community, with movements to new perspectives and terminology, is seen by others as a wrong turn. As I will show, they often accuse the other over what's deemed to be missing and when this happens, the words used can be direct. In such cases, specification can be the small print of turf wars and not especially pleasant.

In/disciplined archived lives

In writing this book, I realized that the potential approaches to the topics raised in thinking about the two disciplines ran in multiple and at times confusing directions, and that I needed my own archive of words that would allow me to make my arguments, especially if the writing is to have clarity and *provoke*, which is part of the job of a volume in this series. The endless detail and cacophony of critical opinion that emanate from all the subjects associated with medicine and disability will inevitably overwhelm any writer and I needed a point of focus that would allow me to use specifics but also maintain the shape of my attempt to think broadly across both disciplines. As I tried to form my ideas and find pathways that might help me, I was asked to review Jan Grue's remarkable memoir of living with spinal muscular atrophy, *I Live a Life Like Yours*, prior to its publication in late 2021. Grue's story of his life is honest and unflinching, laced with philosophy and cannily self-aware of the complexities of disability life-telling. In finding his own way of starting, Grue writes 'This book cannot begin until I have found its language, and by the time the language exists, the book will be finished, and all the work will be done', an observation that very much spoke to me as I struggled with how to put my own language together.[9] Thinking about disability and health always creates the possibility of what Grue calls, beautifully, 'a cathedral of meaning', a powerful, overarching and unavoidable framing of content, however it is constructed. But, he concludes, it is 'a literary sense of logic' that structures the 'archive' of his life, an interesting and possibly surprising observation from a man who is a social scientist with a research specialization in qualitative data.[10] Stories of health, Grue asserts, require the workings of the literary – the writerly need – to bring them to light, to do them justice. As I sought an archive that would make this book possible, Grue's identification of a literary structure to *his* ordering of his experiences resonated with me.

Not only because of the power of Grue's story and his thoughtfulness about its form, I have chosen life stories as my source, the ground beneath this book's feet. In part this is because there is so much of it, whether memoir, comprehensive biography, biopic, VR experience, or online blog and vlog, all articulating health experience. But the choice also makes sense for me because it comes with all the constructive ambiguities inherent in describing those experiences, the messy contradictions, as in all texts, of health and disability lives that as a literary critic I am drawn to. The shape of a lived life is such a powerful frame for the discussion of health, but the arc of being in the world is rarely straightforward, and in my experience it is not a story that proceeds in a manner that is linear or always comprehensible. It is, however, compelling (possibly precisely for these reasons) and each of us has some version of it.

After a first draft that wrestled with the idea of the archive, I turned back to Ann Cvetkovich's book *Depression*, a text that had inspired me before, in which she mixes memoir and academic enquiry to explore what she terms the 'public feeling' of depression. Cvetkovich's method was her attempt to avoid what she calls the 'stuckness' of her own ill health, to find new ways of living and moving, to see a condition as more than private experience and rather as an encounter, search or crossing. It involves using what she calls an 'unconventional archive' in an attempt to uncover a mode of 'reparative scholarly work' that might 'reinvigorate forms of humanities writing that are based in creative and speculative thinking and feeling'.[11] That this could come from the contemplative space of Cvetkovich's own shifting health made perfect sense to me. Reparative is not recovery, not restitution. It is more partial and provisional, more (as Cvetkovich says) speculative. The speculation of the creative is the thinking of the literary and the feeling of the body, and vice versa. It made me more certain of the subject areas in which I work, my own archive, and their indiscipline.

Indiscipline (and then In/Disciplines) became an idea and word that came late in my writing, as its language came to exist. I am drawn to it for a number of reasons: first, it allows for an obvious situating *within* discussions of the disciplinary concerns that necessarily speak of how academic scholarship works in institutional and intellectual spheres; second, it qualifies this location – messes it up – because of its clear suggested unruliness. It places disciplines in recognizable structures but then subjects them to the rule-breaking energy of nonconformity. This is my modest version of Donna Haraway's staying with the trouble or perhaps Bruno Latour's disruptive rebellions but, as Haraway has observed, to be in such a situation is not only to be oppositional, not only *simply* critical. Rather, it heralds a positioning that inhabits spaces of both avoidance and adherence. Outlining her ideas of witnessing, Haraway tells us that her witness 'is suspicious, implicated, knowing, ignorant, worried, and hopeful', heir to the 'cascading accounts' of configurations that write any topic or subject.[12] It is exactly through this kind of doubtful and/but generative lens that I look at the scholarship that mark Disability Studies and Medical Humanities as critical modes. As Matthew Wolf-Meyer has observed, doubt is inherently generative, especially as, even if unwanted, it drives the *processes* of research. But it is also inevitably unsettling and anxiety-inducing.[13] The more I think about research, teaching and thinking across both disciplines, the more I realize that it's impossible to *not* be worried.

As my own work has developed, I have found that being *in*disciplined provides the clearest mode for the criticism I hope to write. This is true despite the apparent *lack* of clarity around the word itself ('indiscipline' is more common that 'undiscipline', but 'undisciplined' more in usage than 'indisciplined'), something I like because it is its own version of 'not otherwise specified'. And what might a book on health and disability make of *ill*-disciplined? Possibly there's a danger here of getting too close to disappearing down Alice's rabbit hole, but I'd like that phrase to be around the edges of the book as well.[14] It's important to stress that this adoption of the provisional and contingent doesn't detract from my desire to shed light on the workings of each discipline and to write with clarity; it's a matter of how and where to start. Overall, I hope that this book, as a provocation, has its fair share of constructive and insightful indiscipline.

As a result, the book is an attempt at a creative criticality, a scholarly contemplation laced with life stories as continual animation. The stories work as examples of my discussion, drive arguments, complicate conclusions (of both 'life' and 'story'), and hopefully serve to make the book the kind of provocation I want it to be. In another mode of writing, they might be described as the spine of the study, the crucial linking between sections that carry different weight. But if they are a spine, they are kinked, problematic as opposed to straightforward, maybe painful but still often ordinary – more like Grue's spine than the majority. It is Hamlet who realizes that 'time is out of joint' when he faces the shape of his life in the light of the death of his father, and we might see the status of life stories as being truth-telling through exactly this productive disjointedness. An idea of being 'out of' is also a necessary partiality, both of detail and language, and of avoidance and leaving. Grue notes: 'I avoid certain words in what I write, there are words I could have used but did not use.'[15] For me, this is what has always united literature, disability and health: all tell of worlds through difficult, partial, avoided and often chaotic forms that nevertheless come together to make truths. I've avoided some words as well, though in other moments I've forced myself to use others that I've probably avoided for too long, for fear they might be problematic.

It is important to stress that these life stories and the archives through which they speak are not only individual. A Euro-American tradition of health narratives is predominantly about personal experience, reflecting the stress such cultures place on the role of the individual and apparently centred self (this is often true even if the illness or disability being recounted offers the suggestion of being *decentred*, because the focus remains on the personal). Stories of struggle, recovery, achievement, pain or trauma usually revolve around how one figure encountered illness or disablement. But this is not how health and disability are always understood; in fact they are relational in so many ways. As such, I want to use life narratives because they proactively *name a world*, even as they emerge from specific origins. Stories include families, loved ones and friends and other communities. In Chapter 1, I read writing by Black women who see their mental ill health as inseparable from the contexts of race that surround them every day; in Chapter 3, I discuss memoirs detailing autoimmune conditions, such as endometriosis and lupus, which build capacity because they acknowledge a shared history of the encounter between women's bodies and healthcare systems. Life writing about menstruation, for example, is rarely presented as a singular act; rather it highlights connections and acts of support. Often these affiliations are more than simply content. Narratives can be co-produced, shared in their creation, and are in some cases meaningful *only* because of their intertwinings. There are numerous cultures that see health in foundational terms as a collective. This is especially common in many Indigenous communities: in New Zealand, the He Korowai Oranga framework builds Māori interactive conceptions of individuals, families and environments into the national health service, as a 'living strategy'; while Himba models of kinship and genealogies in Namibia guide how health is understood as a broad, inclusive category. In addition to these examples, Covid-19 has taught the need to further think of health in terms of knowing community. Understanding the impact of the pandemic on, say, Satmar Hasidic Jewish society in Brooklyn, or Muslim families in Bradford, requires real awareness of the way such groups see health as being more than an experience that affects individuals. It is always structural, always about systems.

In finding this archive of stories, I came to a decision that surprised me: I realized that I wanted to add my own. In fact, because of how I was responding to the contents, particularly the way the book had become a challenge, I felt *provoked* to do so, a realization that then came to feel like a natural fit with the book's other concerns. In my previous writing about disability, I have always argued for the benefits of a critical position that refuses to insist upon clear distinctions between writer and subject. In my case, because of my experiences, that would simply be untrue. And I felt the same again as I began to write here. But the reasons are not only personal. I believe that the anecdote, the story, or the interjection are modes of theory that amplify an academic focus and give it sharpness and depth. Patient stories are often seen as a vital element in assessing or describing health, but I see their power as more than any simplistic sense of being 'given a voice'. I like how they disturb even as they clarify; indeed, they clarify *because* they disturb. It is not only voice that is added when such stories are prioritized: it is affect, presence, form, demand, complaint, misdirection, sometimes courage or despair, among others. I am far from the only writer who relies upon these modes as critical tools because of how they both provide and trouble, but I find them invaluable. Here then are two poems that bookend all the writing and four vignettes, one after the introduction and each chapter. They carry a health or disability encounter I have had at different stages of my life. They are not meant to be confessional – in many ways they are mainly about confusion, doubt and the kind of absent knowledge that makes impossible the integrity offered by an idea of 'confession' – but they helped me in understanding what kind of provocation I want the book as a whole to be. They become an example of a disseminated writing practice, part of the critical story I hope I can marshal, one that I feel I can legitimately call – to pick up on the terminology already mentioned – my own specification when I think about Medical Humanities and Disability Studies. For me, this comes as the result of situating life stories in and through critical frames, and vice versa, letting the words and thoughts and absences collide with one another. I am part of that – it is why and how I think and write – and so the poems and vignettes take their place here, fragments of a memoir maybe, but also part of a theoretical vocabulary, always with a job to do.

Uneasy balances

Moving through words to stories to frames has made me realize that my writing had to engage in what I came to understand as a complicated balancing yet interrogative act. To write on Medical Humanities and Disability Studies as disciplines alone, exploring purely their critical moves, came to strike me as unimaginative and of limited value. Rather, it is crucial to recognize that they are both labels and signposts to things more complex than labelling can ever be; that they are ways of pointing towards the actualities of health and disability. My writing balance needs to hold together the experience and manifestations of health and disability and the terms in which they're expressed, and then discuss the critical approaches and academic disciplines that come to focus on them. The experiences and the critical frames overlap, but of course have their own discrete forms. In what follows, I want to address this balance, especially through the specifics of how of words, stories and frames cascade their meanings and inform the issues that surround experience, bodies, community, objects and reflections. For some, undertaking this might involve focusing work on the human, but my work on posthumanism has made me deeply suspicious of such a category and especially the humanism that goes with it; humanist ideals rarely have space for disability and frequently are problematic for those who are ill. So I see both disability and health as conditions – multiple, complex and overlapping – that are directed towards questioning the meaning of what is constituted by the human even as they might prioritize the word. If *this* meaning – the supposed primacy of the human – is left 'not otherwise specified', then scholarship in the disciplines will be consigned to a profound and far-reaching ignorance, one that applies to disabled and non-disabled, the ill and the well.

The book's title sets parameters for me. Necessarily, I have to explore the *work* undertaken by Medical Humanities and Disability Studies, the disciplines' presence as systems, their terms of reference, the shape of their arguments, and the specific kinds of lenses through which they see their material. These issues are directly connected to the domains – or the archives – on which the two disciplines focus, but they have their own groupings, dynamics, and rules. The disciplines work hard to partner with non-academic communities and connect especially to those who live lives where health and disability are central. At the same time, they are inextricably linked to the contemporary academy. From funding to fellowships, and job titles to journals, research and teaching proceed through the ways that academic institutions contrast modes of participation. It's my intention to always keep the frames of each subject in play as I discuss texts or ideas, so that there is always the presence of *how* each addresses its topics.

Even as I try to do this, I want to attend to the gaps, pauses and vanishing points in both Medical Humanities and Disability Studies and to stress the *in*discipline caused in the best work they produce. I want to avoid the insularity and parochial mood that can come with disciplines as they start to settle, whether within a model of disciplinary formation or taken-for-granted critical perspectives. The fact that at this current moment in time parts of academia choose to frame scholarship in medicine, health and disability within certain terms is a passing phase. It will change and develop in years to come. What won't change is the central role that medicine, health and disability have in people's lives and to the social and cultural formations that surround them. I understand it to be the job of both Disability Studies and Medical Humanities to respond to these issues, to be more than words that designate disciplines, subject areas or the names of postgraduate courses and funding schemes. In fact, I value them precisely because I believe that they can do this. They bring philosophical concepts of selfhood into dialogue with personal experiences of bodily pain, for example, or theorize disabled embodiment as it helps inform systems of social health. To call this inter-, cross- or multi-disciplinary is fine, but only if those words are understood to come *as a response to* the work that finds formation in and around such headings. I agree with Felicity Callard and Des Fitzgerald's suspicions that these terms, for all that they wish to speak of collaboration and complexity, simply move the space of work out of the disciplinary to a place of 'between', 'over' or 'many', and that these then perform their own version of stasis, assumed but often unexamined.[16] As ever, methodologies create their own shortcuts.

Writing this book has been a much more difficult experience than I anticipated. I work within these two disciplines all the time and they are where my brain is located for much of my working day. Straightforward then, to write about the relationship between the two. Yet it has proved anything but. I am normally a confident writer and I trust my judgement and capacity to be articulate when facing the laptop. But there has been much more doubt this time. I have written sentences that I (still) frown at, but I realize that part of the way that this book wants to elicit response is through expressing uncertainty and contradictions; indeed arguing that such uncertainty and contradiction are *necessary* in voicing critical opinions. Some provocations are wonderfully sharp, laser-like in focus and argument, but this has turned out not to be one of those. Possibly because of the need to keep so many interactions in play – all the overlaps, tensions and absences I've tried to describe above – I found that there was no choice but to inhabit a difficult, liminal space. With such a location comes an inevitable uncertainty, a stopping and starting, and to write from such a position involves partiality and the risk of being wrong. At the end of the book, I argue for the usefulness of the concept of agility as a way to practise good criticism through a kind of restless movement, but I do so in the recognition that although it's the argument I want to make, it's unavoidably precarious and open to challenge. Eve Kosofsky Sedgwick once spoke of how writing made her feel 'pressed against the limits of my stupidity' and I fully recognize that.[17] But this is the point towards which this book has naturally worked, so it is the right place for it to be.

The same is true for the question of inclusivity. The difficult and liminal are not spaces from which to offer a broad panoptic vision of how health and disability operate, something that would have been impossible even if that were my intention. So my decision to focus on specific moments and manifestations will offer only limited coverage and (like all other academics) I'm aware of the vast amount of material I have left out. Here I found insight and support from Albert Robillard's *Meaning of a Disability*, his 1997 memoir detailing his Motor Neurone Disease. Robillard notes that he wants to cover as many aspects of his condition as possible, but that 'the reader will have to remember that inclusiveness is a recipient-designed phenomenon. Because I do not know my readers, there may be some whose interests I will miss'.[18] Inclusive is such an important term and concept in Disability Studies, rightly seen as a core principle in research on all aspects of disability experience, but I was struck here by Robillard's stress on the recipient's role, and not the researcher's responsibility, in the creation of the idea. This changes and interrogates the taken-for-granted element of what inclusivity means, shifting it to suggest that at times it depends upon what people *want*. As I continued writing, then, I felt less pressurized to cover everything I thought readers might expect. I want to say things, and though I hope that you want to read them, I understand that you will maybe feel frustrated about what's not included or how it's discussed. A meeting point somewhere will hopefully make things work. In the end, though, provocations are necessarily selective.

Forcing myself to encounter fully the scope and scale of Medical Humanities and Disability Studies has opened to enquiry something I realized that I had, to echo my point above, taken for granted. It has made me return to some core ideas and critical traditions that underpin both disciplines, and to assess them again. It has also brought the doubts I mention here (which turn out to be doubts about the areas themselves as well as my capacity to engage with them) into a better light and demanded that I think them through. That this has worried and destabilized me is a good thing, but it was not what I planned. In part, the idea of agility that I move towards in the conclusion is a recognition of being destabilized and attempt to learn from this, to value movement as a productive product of doubt and uncertainty. For these reasons, I'm pleased that it came late in my writing. As with indiscipline, agility was never part of a thesis or plan, but a concept that arose organically from the book taking certain paths. It's not easy in critical writing, where arguments and evidence are so important, to let exploration find (indeed *make*) its own terms, but that's what happened here.

Conclusion: Complex conceits

In the end, I found the words and form that allowed me to write this book. I found that it's possible to think through the messy presence of each discipline and to structure an argument about their relationship even while acknowledging what is missing, half-said, or repressed. The relationship between Medical Humanities and Disability Studies is often reciprocal and can be generative and vital – and certainly that there are potential spaces to explore this further. At the same time, it is uneven, contradictory, poorly articulated and not infrequently characterized by suspicion or intellectual one-upmanship.[19] There is relatively little writing that compares the disciplines and I find it interesting that, where it does take place, it often originates from Disability Studies scholars who look to show how Medical Humanities needs to benefit from their particular points of view. Work that aims to showcase the reverse is virtually non-existent, despite it being needed. To give one example, in an essay entitled 'Towards a Crip Medical Humanities', Travis Chi Wing Lau writes that 'disability studies is a field uniquely positioned to insist on [an] ethical necessity and critical purchase [. . .] as the medical and health humanities continue to define themselves as fields', adding: 'Exposing and revising medicine's social agendas is precisely what is crip about disability studies and why the medical humanities urgently needs a crip turn.'[20] Disability Studies here gets to insist, with crip the uninterrogated category through which that insistence is to be articulated, and Medical Humanities needs to learn as a matter of urgency.

Put crudely, in such a dialogue Disability Studies displays its progressive credentials and demands Medical Humanities catch up with its history of engagement and theoretical sophistication, while Medical Humanities, sometimes seemingly guilty about its humanist past and insecure about its own methodologies, aims to acquiesce and improve its activist credentials, at times downplaying its own strengths. I caricature here, but not overly so. And it's not that I necessarily disagree with such a perspective – indeed Chapter 2 of this book argues precisely for thinking about medicine through the nuance of crip and other critical disability positions – but I don't agree that scholarship that looks at the relationship between the two disciplines should work like this *alone*. Why not have a critical Medical Humanities investigation of crip, something entirely possible? Crip Theory is a wonderful concept, but it has been around for nearly fifteen years now and has settled to become an orthodoxy that receives little scrutiny; much of the best theoretical work in Medical Humanities, it might be noted, is more recent. A major point that emerges for me from such exchanges – that disability scholars should be more self-reflective and open to other disciplines that talk about medicine, health and bodies – is, I think, an important one.

Suspicion and its consequences can be forms of indiscipline as they work to create room for contestation and revision. As I hope to show, the practices of each discipline can operate in ways that challenge what seem to be the 'successes' of the other, and this particular idea has in fact come to drive much of the thinking in this book. But suspicion can also be hostility, and hostility needs to be handled carefully. In disability encounters especially, hostility is predominantly an expression of prejudice and absence of respect, part of the structure of discriminatory systems that dominate and suppress. It can also be a pushback against these structures, though, as many activists and advocates show.

I am no fan of scholarship that demands speed, or research that is spurred only by short-term challenges, as if thinking is some subset of a rapid response unit. Proclamations that that we 'must' develop thinking in certain directions, that 'the only way to understand …' something is through a certain critical paradigm, or (as in the above example) there is an 'urgent' requirement for certain critics to listen to others, unsettle me: what kind of authority or entitlement is implied in such public expressions? To demand that there have to be synergies or 'learning' between critical approaches to medical, health and disability not only risks flattening out their various perspectives, but also (more importantly) threatens not to do justice to the experiences and worlds they seek to discuss. Assertions of moral superiority and outright dismissiveness do no one any good, but both are found in the work we do. Better maybe to accept that words are inevitably missing, even as (for those of us who find ourselves in the act of writing) words are all that we have. Not seeing this as a contradiction is, in fact, a useful model. It can be extended to see that not all disabled people are unhealthy, and not all ill health is disabling. Equally, not all research routes are profitable and not all disciplines or subject areas name the things they wish to address. Bearing all this in mind isn't always easy, but it's no bad place to start. Despite my surprise in not finding the term Medical Humanities in my disability/ posthuman book, then, it doesn't mean that it isn't there in other forms; and possibly its presence isn't in fact diminished by it not being named. It's what to do with that insight that's important. And that's the thought I want to follow.

In terms of where that thinking goes, I have had to structure what I term above my disseminated writing. Across the three chapters, I focus on what I see as tautologies that surround questions of health and disability, and then explore them as case limits that challenge the parameters of Medical Humanities and Disability Studies scholarship. Finding complex health expressions that do this evolved as a natural way of interrogating both the scope of critical writing produced in each discipline and the relationship between them. It also allows for what I see as a main element of my provocation, namely to take examples where it might be expected that one critical model predominates and show how in fact the other can provide greater insight. So in Chapter 1, ideas of disabled difference are juxtaposed with the power of what I call 'disability same' and, conversely, the commonalities of medical same are seen as unspooling examples of difference. In Chapter 2, the major focus is on life writing about schizophrenia, which I suggest is best understood through a Disability Studies critical frame even though it seems a set of conditions saturated by ideas of 'the medical'. Chapter 3 reverses this, looking at a series of disabling conditions that affect women's bodies – especially endometriosis – and might seem most meaningfully discussed within discourses of disability identity, but are in fact, I argue, illuminated by critical writing in Medical Humanities.

I'm aware that this approach is cryptic, possibly baroque and potentially self-indulgent. It's also a clear critical conceit in which a highly manufactured structure within and across chapters makes arguments that could be made differently (I know this is true for much academic writing, especially in the Humanities – and particularly in English/Cultural Studies – but here it's even more so). But that's what a provocation should aim for, and I found insight in doing it this way. Using one discipline to challenge the working methods of the other not only helped in seeing the limits of each, but also offered a way to unpick the success that each currently enjoys, something I don't think is discussed enough. It's easy to position oneself in critical Humanities' approaches to health and disability, and to have an uninterrogated sense of moral self-importance. That has to be wrong and should be addressed. Doing so is, I think, part of being indisciplined in the ways in which I want this book to be; not only arguing to be provocative, but provoking through methods and perspectives that provide insight. I didn't want to write this book in order to reinforce what I felt I already knew. Part of doing it was to force myself to find new ways of thinking, especially through challenging ideas I (and others) have held for some time.

The poems and reflections are part of this. They provide different kinds of writing that pick up the topics of the chapters that precede them, framing these and helping with the structure of the book overall. So, the first poem begins in childhood and the last is about ageing, while the reflections all centre on experiences – epilepsy, autism, mental health and women's bodies – that have been discussed in some way immediately before, even if they're not named. The aim here is to allow diverse perspectives to work through the ideas raised in each section, but also to have boundaries, however permeable they might be. I would want to make it clear that I see the book as a whole. Everything that comes after the first poem takes place in the shadow it casts and all my ideas flow into the sentiments of the second. In that sense of start and finish, the book isn't complicated at all. It's really pretty straightforward, which is precisely what I hope for.

Notes

1. In writing this book, I struggled with being precise about the difference between a discipline and subject area. Many of the explanations I found seemed to be unsatisfying. So I've gone for a relatively straightforward breakdown: I term both Medical Humanities and Disability Studies disciplines and the critical approaches that fall under their umbrellas – things such as History of Medicine, Narrative Medicine, Philosophy of Care, Sociology of Health etc. – as subject areas. I'd like to thank Clare Barker and Amelia DeFalco for reading and commenting on this Introduction.

2. Benjamin Johnson and Kenneth Levy, 'Personality Disorder Not Otherwise Specified (PDNOS)', in *Encyclopedia of Personality and Individual Differences,* ed. Virgil Zeigler-Hill and Todd K. Shackelford, 1–11. Available online: https://doi. org/10.1007/978-3-319-28099-8_924-1 (accessed 3 March 2020). As Johnson and Levy note: 'Given the paucity of research on PDNOS, much is left unknown regarding the PDNOS diagnosis, its treatment, and the individuals who comprise its ranks' (8); Roel Verheul and Thomas Widiger, 'A Meta-Analysis of the Prevalence and Usage of the Personality Disorder Not Otherwise Specified (PDNOS) Diagnosis', *Journal of Personality Disorders* 18, no. 4 (2004): 309–19. Available online: https://doi.org/10.1521/pedi.2004.18.4.309 (accessed 3 March 2020).

3. P. Tyrer, N. Coombs, F. Ibrahimi, A. Mathilakath, P. Bajaj et al., 'Critical developments in the assessment of personality disorder', *British Journal of Psychiatry* 190, S49 (2006); 423–31 (p. 435); Lee Anna Clark, 'Assessment and Diagnosis of Personality Disorder: Perennial Issues and an Emerging Reconceptualization', *Annual Review of Psychology,* 58 (2007): 227–57 (246).

4. Virginia Woolf, 'On Being Ill', *Selected Essays* (Oxford: OUP, 2008), 102.

5. Joseph Straus, 'Autism as Culture', in *The Disability Studies Reader* (4th edn), ed. Lennard J. Davis (London and New York: Routledge, 2013), 474.

6. *The Guardian,* 23/12/2020. Available online: https://www.theguardian.com/world/2020/dec/23/toronto-van-killer-autism-defence-alek-minassian (accessed 11 February 2021).

7. Kay Redfield Jamison, *An Unquiet Mind: A Memoir of Moods and Madness* (London: Picador, 1996), 181–2.

8. Simi Linton, *Claiming Disability: Knowledge and Identity* (New York and London: New York University Press, 1998), 14–17.

9. Jan Grue, *I Live a Life Like Yours* (London: Pushkin Press, 2021), 75.

10. Grue, *I Live a Life Like Yours*, 140 and 154.

11. Ann Cvetkovich, *Depression: A Public Feeling* (Durham, NC, and London: Duke University Press, 2012), 26. Cvetkovich is a wonderful scholar of the relationship between archives and feelings. See also her book *An Archive of Feelings: Trauma, Sexuality, and Lesbian Public Cultures* (Durham, NC, and London: Duke University Press, 2003).

12. Donna Haraway, *Modest_Witness@Second_Millenium, FemaleMan©_Meets_OncoMouse™* (London and New York: Routledge, 1997), 3 and 2.

13. Matthew Wolf-Meyer, 'What Can We Do with Uncertainty?', *Somatosphere,* 6 February 2018. Available online: http://somatosphere.net/forumpost/what-can-we-do-with-uncertainty/ (accessed 10 October 2022).

14. Thanks to John McLeod for pointing out what had been staring me in the face all along, and letting me borrow it.

15. Grue, *I Live a Life Like Yours*, 227.

16. Felicity Callard and Des Fitzgerald, *Rethinking Interdisciplinarity across the Social Sciences and Neurosciences* (Basingstoke: Palgrave Macmillan, 2015), 80–1. As they also put it succinctly: 'Interdisciplinarity is a term that everyone invokes and none understands', 4.

17. Cvetkovich uses the line as the epigraph for *Depression*.

18. Albert Robillard, *Meaning of a Disability: The Lived Experience of Paralysis* (Philadelphia: Temple University Press, 1999), 2.

19. Sedgwick would call this 'paranoid reading'. See 'Paranoid Reading and Reparative Reading; or, You're So Paranoid, You Probably Think This Introduction Is about You' in *Novel Gazing: Queer Readings in Fiction*, ed. Eve Kosofsky Sedgwick (Durham, NC: Duke University Press, 1997), 1–37.

20. Travis Chi Wing Lau, 'Towards a Crip Medical Humanities', in *Culture and Medicine: Critical Reading in the Health and Medical Humanities*, ed. Rishi Goyal and Arden Hegele (London: Bloomsbury, 2022), 131 and 134.

REFLECTION 1: 342 GREEN

What I really don't want is for it to be someone dressed in green. Because if it is, there's a strong chance that the green in question will be a shade that signals trouble. It's a dark green that's not exciting enough to be quite racing green, not a glossy green in the way that serious academic books were in the 1990s, not bright so as to signal fresh grass. There are other colours that come into focus, notably the hi-vis yellow that you might think might be a dominant impression, but no – Pantone 342 green is the one that gives it away, definitely dark but strangely nondescript.

Blue and white are the colours that 82 per cent of people in the UK associate with the National Health Service, the core colours that dominate everything in hospitals from clothes to signage and stationery. In the NHS's breakdown of its colour identity guidelines, there are in fact five separate 'top level' shades of blue that create tonal variety in emphasising that association. But 342 green denotes the emergency services. It is the paramedic's apparel, the rapid response colour. Technically, it's a support act, chosen because it's close enough to blue in the colour spectrum that anyone seeing it will recognize its relation to NHS blue, but won't feel that it over dominates the primary association that lets blue and white signal 'Medicine'. For me, though, it's up front and very personal. If it's that particular green, then the person standing over me and repeating my name over and over as I open my eyes is almost certainly a member of an ambulance crew and I'm coming to realize that I've just had a seizure.

The point here is not really about my epilepsy and the seizure itself; that's actually something that in many ways I know very little about. It's about finding myself in an ambulance afterwards – because that means I'm on my way to hospital and that something has happened about which I'm unaware. I'm sure I'm not the only person with epilepsy who has this immediate post-seizure double move: first the whole messiness of the thing itself – what hurts, where it happened, what I can remember – and then the realization that instead of just being able to find a corner to sleep it off, I'm going to have to be stuck on a trolley in a corridor or behind a screen somewhere in a busy hospital, surrounded by all the hum and thrum of the accident and emergency department, just wishing for some quiet. 342 green is the first sign of what the next few hours are going to be like.

The time immediately after a seizure is, for me, dominated by a shifting palette of sensory experiences. Lights are too bright, sounds too loud; a hospital emergency room is in fact about the worst place I could be. Stranger is the onset of a longer-term, almost synaesthetic overlapping of some of these experiences, or feel of memories. Once, after a morning seizure, I spent the rest of the day and much of those that followed having powerful memories of an academic conference I'd attended, years before, in Belgium. The memories were visceral, not just sights, sounds and tastes, but a profound feeling of place and of presence. It was unsettling to find myself walking down everyday streets at home but experiencing an overwhelming sensation of being in another country.

This shifting sideways begins quite early during the first recovery from a seizure. Because of the tonic phase, in which the muscles contract violently, my body afterwards can feel as if it's had an intensive, very painful, workout, something heightened by the flush of blood that rushes through my skin. Once, when looking in the bathroom mirror after a morning seizure in which I'd cut my head and had blood smeared across my face, I honestly thought that I looked like extra character in Fight Club, *a novel I was writing on at the time. On those days where I would have a second seizure in the afternoon (a mid-morning/late-afternoon split was always my version of this), I would have a strange, inchoate sense of anticipation – a coming-to that was also a waiting for the inevitable – and it felt like being pulled back into this world of physical extremities.*

For psychotherapist and manipulative memoirist Lauren Slater, epilepsy is all about the fall. The condition, she writes, is 'a dangerous disease because you can hurt yourself crashing down, and so you have to learn to crash', a comment I'm fond of because it both make sense and doesn't. You can anticipate the crash – I would sometimes wear my worst coat to work because if I'm going to end up lying in the road or on a station platform, there's no point wearing the good one; keep my phone in my pocket because if it's in my hand it could end up anywhere – but in my experience you can't actually learn it. The bang is too sudden, impossible to prepare for even if, with hindsight, you can see signs: a lack of clarity in thought or confusion in finding the right language just before the seizure itself. Slater adds that 'I think secretly each and every one of us longs to fall, and knows in a deep wise place that surrender is the means by which we gain, not lose, our lives' and continues 'I liked to fall. It gave me so much confidence, so much pride. I was good at it and I knew, even though I could never have said it, that the falling skill was widely generalizable, that I would be able to use it in love, use it in fear, use it in hope'; which is great because it's so typical of the wonderful way she writes. It's both profound and provocatively nonsensical, positive in asserting agency but becoming gloriously absurd.[1]

But the fall is the major part I've never known. Like other moments I've addressed in the Introduction, it's missing. I piece together the actual details of my seizures through what others tell me – the noise I make at the start when the air is pushed out of my lungs, how I twist to the right, the convulsions my body makes when it's on the ground. Consciousness and questions kick in as the recovery starts and I return.[2] *The fall itself – the central act and extra-ordinary drama of it all – is for the consumption of those who are there; a large part of it is outsourced. I may make it but others get to judge the performance. I've had seizures in all sorts of situations: when carrying £2,000 in cash to pay into a bank for an employer for whom I'd been working for two days (this was my first, when I was twenty-one); the evening after an interview for an academic job; in a beautiful, book-lined eighteenth-century room at a British Academy invitation-only exhibition; in a hospital maternity unit shortly before the birth of my son; right outside the emergency department of one of the largest hospitals in northern Europe, only then to be ferried across town to another hospital for logistical reasons. But the memories are never of this because they're always post-fall. They're far less interesting. Being helped down the wonderful wide central staircase at the British Academy by paramedics while the exhibition attendees looked at me and maybe wondered if I'd been in a fight is not the glamorous descent I might have wished for.*

I make sense of my seizures through mechanisms that knit them in patterns. One of these is possibly the most obvious, a storyline that puts them into a narrative, but I sometimes think of them as group activities that can involve family, friends, and strangers. Often it's this last group that interests me the most, the people I never see, the missing: those who call the ambulance when I fall in the street; the passengers forced to wait on a train (for how long?) on one occasion after it had to stop between stations and wait for me to be picked up; or the people who took the cash to the bank when they saw the paying-in slip. These really are missing: they can only be presumed, made from the evidence of others when I recount the pieced-together story, but I know that they must have been there. Who they were and what they did intrigues me. Were they frightened? Did they immediately switch to care mode? Did they go home and tell their loved ones all about it? It would be nice to specify something about them, but I can't – beyond conjecture and imagination, and gratitude. It's a kind of anti-evanescence, a willed passing into existence and memory of something that was there and not. Making missing meaningful.

After having two seizures in hospital following my first admission, I was told by a doctor that having epilepsy was very serious and would affect all aspects of my life. I'd have to think about what job I did, where I lived, and how my relationships would work. It was difficult to take in and I remember feeling that I should have experienced the moment as more profound than I did (possibly this was due to medication). A diagnosis that writes a life-long, but at the same time unimaginable, future felt light, too difficult to comprehend fully. There was a meaningful space that was at the same time a void without detail, full and missing all together. As it was bound to, life went on, sometimes with seizures, nearly all the time without them. A point that I have realized in writing this book is that experiencing a disability or health condition – having one, living one – doesn't necessarily mean knowing it, for all that you might be the source. I think this is important because so much to do with health revolves about the issue of claim: claiming selfhood or an identity, claiming to be sick when others doubt you, claiming rights and benefits. Does my epilepsy give me a space from which to claim? Does it make me disabled? At times I think yes, but mostly, no. Overall, seriously, I don't know.

I have had seizures and been taken to hospital in more than one country, but I can't remember if the first colour I saw on these occasions was green, or something else. Although other aspects of the events have stayed in my mind, these details haven't. I could find out, though – could have done so in the course of writing this book – but I chose not to. I left the information out there somewhere, reclaimable maybe, waiting to fall into place.

Notes

1. Lauren Slater, *Lying* (London: Penguin, 2001), 48–49, 51 and 55. Here Slater is somewhat breathlessly discussing how her seizures and falling took place in the context of her resistance to her mother and placement in a special school run by nuns. Later in the memoir, she tells the reader that she might actually not have epilepsy.

2. It seems that I often try to get up and say that I have to go to work, to a meeting or to teach.

CHAPTER 1
MEDICAL/DISABLED, DIFFERENT/SAME

Formations

As with any other critical academic discipline or subject area, both Medical Humanities and Disability Studies have histories and trajectories. I don't want to give too much space to an outline of these here, because others have done so and this isn't a book that has that kind of approach as its focus. In addition, I concur with the editors of *The Edinburgh Companion to the Critical Medical Humanities* that the best way to approach the discipline is not through its history and identity, but rather its imaginary, the various scenes it unfolds (an observation also true for Disability Studies).[1] At the same time, it's important to have a sense of how each operates. So, we might want to know some basics: what were the origins of the disciplines and how do they carry these legacies into their current work? Where are their boundaries? What's included and excluded? Who does the work? And how does this scholarship overlap with other modes of critical enquiry (both old and new)? What kinds of spaces are made for the work to take place – within the academy, the wider intellectual community, and with the public? What feels important, and what is ephemeral?[2]

One context for these questions might be to note that, relatively speaking, each discipline constitutes a highly specialized community, with a limited audience, and that these are unequal in size. Most people who work on literature and medicine, or the history of medicine (to select just two examples) do not identify as Medical Humanities scholars, and for all its profile, the discipline is undoubtedly niche in wider Humanities approaches to health. Disability Studies is more broadly established, with more scholarship having produced a greater number of publications and designated teaching programmes in academic institutions, but it is a subject absent from many universities (in some historical cases because of resistance from 'progressive' academic factions) and other intellectual approaches to disability and healthcare don't engage with its methodologies.[3] In addition, for all that each discipline claims an inter- or multidisciplinary approach to its subject matter, it can be argued that this is restricted in its reach, selecting some partners but dismissing others. Sometimes, I feel that these issues of scale and scope are ignored in discussions about how the disciplines function.

The relationship between medicine and the Arts is centuries old but, as mentioned in the Introduction, Medical Humanities as a distinct discipline emerged in the US from the 1970s onwards as an additional element in the training of doctors and medical professionals. It brought together discussions of literature, creative writing, anthropology, ethics and the visual arts in particular to give new perspectives on questions of (among others) patient experience and behaviour, empathy, professional bias, and cultural difference. The subject still functions primarily in this way in the US, with a strong presence in undergraduate and graduate teaching programmes within medical schools. The emphasis on 'additional' is central here, given that it's a word that has meant different things at different times. When first embedded in medical training, the Humanities offered humanist perspectives on clinical processes and opportunities to engage with alternative ways of talking about health. These were not without interest (sometimes significant) but largely peripheral and clearly a secondary set of perspectives.

The discipline has diversified over the last ten years in particular, developing wider interests and more sophisticated ideas of personal, historical, public and social dimensions of health and mobilizing new critical approaches that address these. But much of the diversity exists with the continuity of the older model. A read-through of the website of the University of California San Francisco's comprehensive and influential *Perspectives in Medical Humanities* series showcases books, digital magazine and podcasts that focus on all manner of topics – from poetry and memoir to studies of cancer and climate change, histories of Obstetrics and Gynaecology, and the structures of medical research finance. The Press's mission statement makes clear, however, that the series invites 'scholars from the humanities and health care professions to share narratives and analysis on health, healing, and the contexts of our beliefs and practices that impact biomedical inquiry', an approach recognizable from the discipline's origins in the 1970s.[4] Similarly, Routledge's book series *Advances in the Medical Humanities* contains multiple titles – on Bioethics, Wellbeing, Palliative Care, Pain, Storytelling and Poetry – almost all of which are connected in some way to Medical Education and person-centred healthcare. It's instructive to note that 2016 saw the publication of both *The Edinburgh Companion to the Critical Medical Humanities*, mentioned above, and Alan Bleakley's *Medical Humanities and Medical Education: How the Medical Humanities Can Shape*

Better Doctors, in the Routledge series. It would be different to imagine two more different books with the same central term in their title.

The Introduction to the *Edinburgh Companion* begins with a claim that, as a discipline, Medical Humanities 'names a series of intersections, exchanges and entanglements'.[5] In so doing, the volume marked part of a major critical turn that reconfigured the subject not as an additional element or 'critical friend' to wider research in medicine and health, but as a seminal part of such approaches. It championed a sustained interdisciplinary inquiry that could not only bring new readings of health moments (of all kinds) but also enact structural change to a research environment. What was before just the *presence* of other subject areas now became critique, articulated through a variety of theoretical models and directed at the positions and presumptions of biomedical science, clinical practice, and healthcare more generally. The subject's imaginary has become a force field of approaches to the full range of medical and health effects.[6]

Like Medical Humanities, Disability Studies originated in the 1970s, led by activists in disability-rights movements and others who rejected the idea that disability should be seen predominantly as a medical issue. In place of this, they championed the rights of disabled people and stressed central social concepts – inclusion, equality, accessibility, discrimination – that marked day-to-day disability lives. Initially focused on physical impairment, the movement spread to include those with neurological conditions and learning disabilities and became characterized by a strong commitment to community, advocating affiliation in place of the estranging individualism frequently forced on disabled people within modes of medical assessment and healthcare. The social model of disability – the acknowledgement that it is social and environmental factors that disable, and not the difference of the disabled body – took specific institutional forms in the 1980s and remains one of the most powerful critical tools in the discipline.

Disability Studies has also had a critical turn, one – again, like Medical Humanities – marked by the advent of multiple theoretical perspectives and new subject methods. The central status of the social model, rooted in specifics of activism, social policy and law, has lessened, with the discipline broadening into fields of Cultural and Literary Studies, as well as Gender, Queer and Critical Race Studies. This is not simply a case of scholars from the Humanities coming to a discipline based in the Social Sciences, but also academics within subject areas such as Sociology and Education continuing the engagement with (particularly) Philosophy and Critical Theory that has been part of their analysis of disability experiences for decades.[7] Like

Medical Humanities, Disability Studies in the last ten to twelve years has brought a greater multidisciplinary approach to focus on the concept of the 'human' that underpins so much thinking about disability and health, and both disciplines criss-cross the promise and problems of contemporary critical topics – care, dependency, contested identities, Posthumanism, digital societies – as they affect the lives of disabled people.

Whether through asserting agency or a commitment to complicating methodologies, then, each discipline asserts the value of reading and championing difference. Medical Humanities wants to bring different critical perspectives to the study of medicine and health, and promote the value of partnerships beyond professional, healthcare and patient groups; Disability Studies stresses difference as well, working through the positive and generative nature of disability experience to provide theories and models of practice that centre around disability inclusion and the value of disabled lives. Scholars in each recognize that the ongoing complexities of health and disability need critical categories themselves capable of multiplicity. Seeing a need for difference is one thing, however; practising it is something different altogether.

Thinking differently

The above emphasis on difference prompts a question: what's the difference of difference? Or maybe it should be: what difference does difference make? Though it's clearly a knotty formation, I've found myself encountering this thought a lot as I've worked on disability especially over the years. I say 'encountering', with its slight stress on the provisional, because I suspect now that I've left the question too much at the edge of my mind, possibly not confident that I have skills to properly address its complexity. I use the term 'disabled difference' a lot. 'It's when we use the insight derived from disabled difference . . .' is exactly the (clumsy) start of a sentence I might write. But what exactly do we mean when we talk about physical, disabled, cognitive, neurobehavioral *difference*? There are easy enough answers of course: a wheelchair-user's experience is different from one that doesn't involve a wheelchair; seeing and encountering a space through OCD is different to doing the same without having the condition. But, while true, this has come to strike me as a pedantic statement of the position. Pedantry thrives on its presupposition of clarity, but frequently simplifies things in order to do so. The assumption that a wheelchair experience is predominantly oriented around a wheelchair, for example, is a simplification of a complex set of relationships in which the wheelchair itself is only one part. That it is the part that *most* signals difference should be an argument, not a given.

The academic world of Disability Studies often involves being inside this difference for most of the time. It stresses the complexities and inequities of being made peripheral (others, maybe yourself) while intellectually inhabiting and critically reassessing the very idea of periphery. Indeed, it stresses that it is precisely in learning about, reforming and reclaiming such space that various productive moments – progressive politics, intellectual insight and creativity, to name just some – become possible. Lennard J. Davis' seminal 1995 text *Enforcing Normalcy: Disability, Deafness and the Body* is a classic example of this, identifying the ableist properties of the category of 'normal' as it has functioned in the modern period, but also noting that 'a society of disabled people can and does easily survive and renders "normal" people outsiders'.[8] Being without allows for the perspective that can critique within, a tactic common in academic methodologies that advocate for social change.

My claim, however, is that at times in Disability Studies the assertion of such difference arguably stops being different and instead becomes a location of assumed knowledge and confident critical superiority. How much is really at stake when an academic professes that disabled difference changes the world? Especially when that academic is almost always implicated in the complex location of the kind of institution which has a problematic relationship with its disabled staff and students (I've never known an exception to this). It is not that academics don't realize this, and much excellent work has been produced on what Sharon Snyder and David Mitchell term the often-precarious 'cultural locations' of disability, both physical and intellectual;[9] but at the same time the world of Disability Studies can become a space in which to say 'disabled difference' is a go-to statement free from risk, a comforting assertion of progressive liberalism.

This hasn't always been the case. In the late 1990s, Simi Linton noted how the emergence of Disability Studies worked as a 'strategic endeavour', a corrective to 'the constricted, inadequate, and inaccurate conceptualizations of disability that have dominated academic inquiry'.[10] Here, the work was that of interlopers, the proud carriers of freak flags with PhDs and the forthright energy to ask questions about curricula and systemic exclusion in and beyond the academy. To think about the twenty-five years since is to highlight a feature this book will return to, namely the complex consequences of the *success* that (first) Disability Studies and (then) Medical Humanities have achieved as disciplines. The process of bringing into critical focus that which has been misunderstood and excluded, and revising the working methods of older disciplines by suggesting new approaches, is clearly a necessity. Likewise, rethinking research topics and methodologies – of all kinds – through diversity and inclusion is essential. But there are dangers that come with such innovation. In terms of new disciplines, innovation can become credentials in showcasing academic relevance, allowing for the jumping of the queue in seeking resources: jobs, funding and institutional opportunities more generally. These processes may wear the clothes of difference, may be firmly committed to it, but paradoxically they can often become a new wave of the same.

I first trained within the emerging discipline of Postcolonial Studies in the 1980s and began my career working in that area. Potential parallels with Disability Studies (especially) have often been on my mind in the years that critical Humanities approaches to disability and health have developed and prospered. This will be a point of contestation for many, but I feel that I watched elements of postcolonial critical thinking lose the energy and novelty of its approaches in its first decades and turn into ways in which the academy absorbed provocative disciplines in a manner that helped contain otherness. The early success of Postcolonial Studies opened up Euro-American institutions to new articulations of global cultures and societies, but arguably the discipline came to exemplify the ways in which difference became consolidated in subject areas (in particular) across universities in those locations; in my experience, scholars rarely actually wrote for readers in the societies and cultures they discussed. There were clear benefits: would anyone argue that, for example, the study of postcolonial literatures revitalized English departments across the globe from the 1980s onwards, introducing new writers and texts to students? But would anyone contest that in 2023 we still need to talk more effectively about race, to decolonize research practices and curricula, to work harder to understand the global? I'm clearly implicated in this and to a degree should know how and why it happened, but I must confess to still feeling bewildered that my own commitment to extending diversity (teaching writing by Pacific, African, Caribbean and South Asian writers for example, or conducting research into Indigenous filmmaking) has ended up framed within a discipline that can be seen to have *limited* the disruptive power – the productive difference – of such work.

This is a point about structures, of course. I still feel that the texts themselves carry that power, but that both critical thinking (theorizing, conferences) and institutionalization (syllabi, curricula, the diversity of the workforce and wider (non)opportunities for career progression) created a quietude where there had been productive troubling. The thought that lingers with me is whether, in its continued success, Disability Studies especially might follow a similar trajectory, that we might be in a moment when Linton's agitators become standard equality curriculum reform memos. And when I say 'we', I again acknowledge that I'm speaking of myself: a white, male, occasional postcolonialist who is now a white, male, sometime-disabled scholar of disability, medicine and health; someone directly involved in the institutional structures mentioned here.

At the same time, it can be simple to characterize agitation and the championing of difference as straightforward forms of an uninterrogated critical force for good. It is common to end an academic event or argument with a call for more radical thinking, as if that were something agreed and understood rather than an admission that this is an incredibly difficult process or fanciful wish (something rarely acknowledged when the downfall of capitalism is called for in the closing session of a conference). Radical agitation can be as closed and blinkered as the causes it seeks to oppose, another version of the same. In today's social-media-saturated world, where a Tweet can make anyone a pariah, disability itself is one of the subjects that nudges close to the you-can't-say-that third rail of self-appointed progressivism that marks academic and public social discourse, with its firm sense of what constitutes justice and demand for appropriate experiential expertise when approaching the topic. Outrage is pervasive on such platforms, and prejudice against disabled people common, but this doesn't mean that the disability-positive version of such commentary should be excused its no-exceptions intolerance.[11] There is a lot of claiming around as to who can and can't speak on what topic and while there are countless vital and progressive arguments that have been possible through claims articulated in this way, particularly by those who lack access to more mainstream media outlets, it's clear that numerous debates are in fact typified by the shared intolerance of the antagonists. Entitlement takes many forms and those who want to propound difference can easily end up enacting the same.

There are any number of examples in academic and academic discourse where difference can become same, then. But there are more important and complex manifestations of disability/same continuities. When Jan Grue says 'I live a life like yours', he is noting that many aspects of his life – studying, getting a job, having a partner, starting a family – are part of the fabric of all sorts of lives. And for Grue, his disability is itself a same: his condition is congenital, and he has never known a life without the body he has. Grue shows that Linton's assertion of the right to claim is not only a claim to the status of being disabled, which, he is careful to assert, can be a time of fear or grief; it's also another format of claiming sameness, that which is unique in the everyday and mundane.

This kind of disability same is everywhere. It permeates lives lived, emotions, hopes and aspirations. There's a nice story told – I don't know its source – of a woman who uses a wheelchair and wants a new kitchen fitted. When the conversations around design start, she is asked what kind of kitchen she wants and replies: 'one that's nicer than my friends'. It's a good twist, personal one-upmanship being more important than what we as listeners might expect: access, adjustments, augmentation. And when the desire is revealed, of course, it's really no surprise at all, because why wouldn't this be a first reaction? In this sense, when it is understood as part of the fabric of everyday life, disability same is powerful and progressive, taking its place as opinion, preference and gesture, naming and commenting on the world.

A complexity, even a tautology, kicks in here. It's precisely a demand for 'same' in disability encounters that underpins ableism. In this formation, same is active in *repressing* disability meaning in that it enacts a retreat from difference to ignorance and intolerance. Here's the challenge for disability scholarship's use of difference, then, one where the very idea begins to creak under the pressure of the work its doing. As the above anecdote demonstrates, disabled difference folds into and around – but doesn't necessarily replicate – how *any* body and mind might work in the world. Collapsing disability into a wider idea of 'bodily difference' is a dangerous relativism that misunderstands how power works. But at the same time, there *is* an interweaving of difference/same through disabled and non-disabled experience, the naming of which can only help in expressions of disability recognition and justice. Lennard J. Davis speaks to this in his collection of essays *Bending Over Backwards*, where he asserts in the title of the book's Introduction that 'People With Disability: They are You', an argument about same he develops with reference to an increasingly ageing global population for which disability will become a fact of life. At the same time, Davis embraces disability as an unstable 'difficult position' (a term in his book's subtitle) exactly *because* of the difference it produces. Such 'difficulty', he asserts, could provide both a new ethics of the body and an identity position that can be a link between others (he mentions race, gender and sexual orientation) in a fully multicultural patterning. This is, Davis acknowledges, highly ambitious, but is nevertheless an example of what he believes that a critical mobilization of disabled difference could do.[12]

Michele Friedner is even more explicit about the interconnections between different and same in her study *Valuing Deaf Worlds in Urban India*, which analyses deaf communities in Bangalore. Friedner notes that a common greeting between deaf people in the city is '*deaf deaf same*', a phrase that means 'I am deaf, you are deaf, we are the same'. '*Deaf deaf same*', she notes, is 'a common sentiment and statement in Bangalore's deaf worlds, and it is a way of expressing deaf similitude or a shared language of being in the world based on common sensorial experience, use of sign language, and an awareness that structural barriers exist for deaf people'. A feeling of '*deaf deaf same*', she continues, interacts with deaf people's circulation through space and locations to produce what she terms 'deaf turns'. At the same time, Friedner develops an idea of 'deaf development' that is geared towards a drive for social equality, something that 'will result in deaf people's becoming equal to normal people – though it will not result in their becoming the same'.[13] Difference and same are held in a complex interrelationship here, one where the concepts of development and turn mark movements in how each operates (I especially like the suggestion of turning towards/away/ between different and same). And crucially the idea is disability led, in that '*deaf deaf same*' is the origin (Friedner employs it at the very start of the book) of the development that reaches out for equality, and therefore justice. This careful charting of the interweaving of difference and same gives a depth of meaning to each as well as the relationship between the two.

We can learn much from these examples then, and avoid falling into the flat uselessness of saying that all bodies are the same because they're different in some way, or that our 'common humanity' means we're all the same despite what are obviously vast differences in experiencing the world. We can learn to respect the particularities of disability and ill health without pushing (or pulling) these so far away that they become fearful or exotic. They can be recognizable, from within and without, even as they weave within and without together. To bring up again an idea that I will make more of in this book's Conclusion, they can be agile, performative and meaningful in the best sense. Agility here is a critical perspective that combines perception and movement, a way of enacting the vision that Davis sees in how similarities and difference can be difficult, and a foundational component in Friedner's concept of the turn.

Same old new

This agile notion of difference/same and the ways they are expressed in both the experiences of lives lived in health and disability and the new academic disciplines that have come to coalesce around them are major elements in this book. They speak to and of the multiple poles/not poles, dualisms/not dualisms that shift and oppose, compliment and contradict, inform and challenge our efforts to make sense of what these essential labels – medicine, disability, health – mean when we come to speak and write them. In the light of this, the book's contents are my attempt to specify arguments and offer agile interventions, knowing that these lie over the missing words of each related topic, the indisciplined and palimpsestic presences that inform understanding but also always suggest possible erasure, helpful signposts and challenging shadows. Aiming to provoke in this context involves finding fluid intersections even while admitting that these might also be powerful oppositions – and wanting to do justice to both in their full manifestations.

Hence my chapter titles, which push words together to show their obvious links, but also (hopefully) to momentarily disorient, to make a reader need a second thought as to how the terms are lined up and what the order might mean. This is an early provocation and hopefully a challenge that also signals the indiscipline that is at the heart of the book. Critically, there is nothing new in observing that dualities have unstable poles and work as continuums as much as contraries; it is a mode that drives theoretical framing and works to recognize nuance and sophistication. But to assert an indisciplined approach to disability and medical contexts of difference/same is to engage with a different critical process, one that is not only a critical paradigm but addresses vital and sensitive elements of health, agency and personhood. After all, there is significant space between a health condition designated as clearly 'different' to the majority of the population and a health status figured as the same as, or consistent with, that majority. With disability, this is equally acute: here, difference is an essential category for multiple reasons, whether in terms of self-image and agency, (non) acceptance by others or access to benefits and allowances. For health and wider state bureaucracies, if a disabled person is deemed to be the same as others, their very status in society can be called into question. Equally, public perception of such a person is unlikely to register their disability experience. To be the same is not to be disabled.

It is an act of indiscipline, then, to argue for a greater interweaving of difference and same. It is a provocation to assert that ill health should not always be understood to be a medical outlier, or that disability is not difference. I want to argue for the specific forms this takes when the topics are not only medicine and disability, but also Medical Humanities and Disability Studies. Most stories of health lives and their contexts never come near academic disciplines, but the latter claim a stake to discuss the former and uses complex critical tools that make this happen. To argue for disability same is to confront some of the politics of identity positioning Disability Studies holds dear; to do something similar with health is to contest one of the very premises of treatment. But, as the following chapters will show, ways that health services treat difference are themselves frequently problematic; and academic study of disability is (surprisingly) often less open and tolerant than might be expected.

Following these trajectories has led me to a series of indisciplined encounters that produce new provocations: on the complexities of claiming; the critical power of cynicism and anger; the prevalence of sneering condescension; the limitations of theory; the structures of listening; and the shortcomings of what might appear to be critical acuity and disciplinary success. Take one of these as an example: listening. Especially in the critical communities in which I find myself, listening presumes the value of a process that extends from the assessment of any given situation or experience to the delivery of what that assessment means. Listening – to a patient or a disabled person – is a good, a foundational, element in Medical Humanities and Disability Studies scholarship.[14] Yet frequently such an assessment is inattentive to exactly how structures obfuscate the very idea of such 'delivery' and here listening can become a gesture, an act that doesn't move on from its initial, well-intentioned, formation. I'm as pleased as anyone who lives with or cares about disability that we talk more about it in the (UK) culture in which I live, that there are more disabled people on television and children's books and that as a result we, as societies and cultures, reach out, listen and try to understand disabled lives. Equally, I welcome any initiative to talk more, and better, about mental health (especially as someone who teaches young people). And yet, the systems of the worlds in which many of us reside continue to disempower those whose bodies or minds signal alternative ways of being in or experiencing the world. Demands to be a certain kind of individual, to move at a certain pace and produce in certain kinds of ways, are as pervasive as ever and to fall ill, have or acquire a disability is to be placed outside of what are incredibly powerful and seemingly unstoppable narratives of personal and communal worth. What spaces are there for those who face a future in which acceptance appears to be welcomed but who are excluded by structures? At times, this feels more insidious than blatant ignorance because it creates what appears to be an attitude of care. Often, cruelly, it can begin with listening.

The offer of the same then, of inclusion, understanding, and welcoming, masks what in fact is frequently an ongoing stress on the kind of difference that is intolerant, that excludes and (at worst) actively punishes. Individuals might be championed, but categories and populations are allowed to fall away. In social and political contexts, these latter remain under-resourced, with care budgets and community services always high on any list of austerity cuts. Likewise the presence of (for example) mental ill health as a subject of agreed social concern doesn't translate into meaningful support for those whose health is so affected. What, put bluntly, can Medical Humanities and Disability Studies *do* about this? Do they, indeed, want to work with these subjects in mind? Maybe to even ask this is to misunderstand the trajectories of their disciplinary concerns as they are manifest in those who work under their umbrellas. It would be cruel to find that the disciplines themselves are examples of the welcoming/exclusion dyad.

Indisciplined lives

I have tried to follow the consequences of thinking about indisciplined and provocative difference/same through the ideas I discuss above. As my thoughts about listening might suggest, my suspicion of individualism and humanism means that in this book I'm not reading life writing because it is the product of singular viewpoints, but rather because it is structural and enacts, to repeat the point I made in the Introduction, the naming of a world. In my view, the best life stories do not claim to supply a veracity of individual experience but work through the recognition of systems and sly mechanics of fabrication and editing, often taking the individual self out of truth and breaking down its centrality as the agent of worth. If this sounds counterintuitive, then I hope that I can show that it isn't. And it's not only an assertion I might make: it's there in the content and indeed the very titles of some of the best books that discuss disability and ill health. Lauren Slater's self-styled 'metaphorical' memoir *Lying*, mentioned earlier and the source of the epigraph for the poem that starts this book, is, as she tells the reader, 'a slippery, playful, impish, exasperating text, shaped, if it could be, like a question mark';[15] Bassey Ikpi's collection of essays on her experience of being Bipolar, *I'm Telling the Truth, but I'm Lying*, captures the same logic. The titular tension here includes not only Ikpi's disjointed immersion into mental ill health, but also the inherent contradiction in any claim that writing of such an experience offers a truth-telling clarity. As she says, 'Lying is how I survive this [...] I lie to control the narrative'. What she terms 'parceling truth' is the survival mechanism that lets her 'walk though this world vacillating between existing and not existing'.[16]

In the memoir of her depression, *Willow Weep For Me*, published in 1998, Meri Nana-Ama Danquah makes precisely this point about world-naming when she observes the ways in Black women are subject to specific structural stigmas in relation to mental health:

> Stereotypes and clichés about mental illness are as pervasive as thought about race. I have noticed that the mental illness that affects white men is often characterized, if not glamorized, as a sign of genius, a burden of cerebral superiority, artistic eccentricity – as if their depression is somehow heroic. White women who suffer from mental illness are depicted as idle, spoiled, or just plain hysterical. Black men are demonized and pathologized. Black women with psychological problems are certainly not seen as geniuses; we are generally not labelled "hysterical" or "eccentric" or even "pathological". When a black women suffers from a mental disorder, the overwhelming opinion is that she is weak. And weakness in black women is intolerable.[17]

Facing her own illness, Danquah saw structure everywhere. No part of her depression escaped the fact she was Black. Even the central metaphors given to medical illness' manifestations – 'A black hole; an enveloping darkness; a dismal existence through which no light shines; the black dog' – became markers of race. 'But', she adds, 'what does darkness mean to me, a woman who has spent her life surrounded by it? The darkness of my skin; the darkness of my friends and family'. For Danquah, 'Depression offers layers, textures, noises' but it is not constituted through blackness: 'It is loud and dizzying, inviting the tenors and screeching sopranos of thought, unrelenting sadness, and the sense of impending doom. Depression is all of these things to me – but darkness, it is not.' Later in her memoir she writes: 'I despise the way blackness, in the English language, symbolizes death and negativity. Because I believe that the absorption of these connotations contributes to self-hate, I avoid them at all cost.'[18] Compare this to one of the most famous memoirs of depression, novelist William Styron's *Darkness Visible* (written in 1990, just a few years before *Willow Weep for Me*) which charts a journey from darkness into light, from 'hell's black depths' to the 'shining world' of health.[19]

Styron's book is firmly focused on an idea of self, detailing the terror that comes when it is lost, and the power of the individual to reclaim it. Danquah complicates all this: she tells her readers that 'Many names and skins have been shed in order for me to evolve into the person I now am'.[20] Born Mildred Mary Nana-Ama Boakyewaa Brobby in Ghana, and called Nana-Ama as a child, she became Mildred Brobby after moving to the US. 'In the face of people who were not part of the culture that I had come to know as my own', she writes, 'my public name and, ultimately, my public persona became Mildred, the English name I was given at birth [...] It hung strangely on my bones, but it was what was given to me so I took it and absorbed all that it was until even my flesh became redolent of its ugliness.'[21] But Mildred transformed into Mary when Danquah was still a child, because 'I convinced myself that only a plain, simple "American" name could provide me with what I wanted most desperately: the luxury of slipping into a void of invisibility'.[22] As a student, Danquah changed her name again when Mary felt unsatisfactory: 'I didn't want to be bland and anonymous anymore. I wanted to be myself – whatever that was. I toyed with the name, exchanging letters here and there, until I arrived at Meri. When I looked at the name *Meri Danquah*, something inside clicked. I felt as if I already owned it.' Reworking her first name and taking her mother's maiden name, after twenty years Danquah found a name that 'wasn't a persona. It was me, who I had been all along'.[23]

Name changes such as these are not unusual in immigrant families. They often signal issues of race, ethnicity or nationality and how these are adjusted following a move to societies unsettled by difference (hence Danquah's reference to skins and the internalized ugliness produced by systemic racism). But, as she makes clear in the discussion of her name, Danquah associates this with her depression and the ways in which it created a disassociation of selfhood – the 'void of invisibility' – that affected both mind and body. She mentions the name changes near the start of a section entitled 'Ghosts at the Edge of a Swamp', which details a return to the neighbourhood in which she grew up. Ghosts, and especially haunting oneself, occur frequently in women's memoirs about their health (I will return to this in Chapter 3); for Danquah, they are manifestations of the 'uncertainty and self-hatred' she experience on her arrival in the US, experiences that she links explicitly to her depression.[24]

Danquah's testimony is another example of the difference of difference (here, the way in which the structural dynamics of understanding mental illness are so often exclusionary of specific experiences) but also difference as same (the way that illness is, for Danquah, always framed within the endlessly repeating tropes of stereotypes about being Black; racism means that her difference is nothing like Styron's).[25] It is the figuration of her depression that speaks to and informs the realities of her Blackness, and vice versa, and this then spills out into the world she names in her memoir. When she reads in a newspaper that a significant number of Black people suffer from depression, she immediately counters with 'But why wouldn't there be?', continuing:

> Depressive disorders do not discriminate along color lines, people do. People determine what is publically acceptable and what is not, who may behave in what way at which time and under which circumstances; and these social mores spill into our private lives, into the images we create. White people take prescription drugs with gentle, melodic names; they go to therapy one or twice a week in nice, paneled offices. Black people take illicit drugs with names as harsh as the streets on which they are bought. We build churches and sing songs that tell us to 'Go Tell It on the Mountain.' Either that or we march. Left, right, left, from city to city, for justice and for peace. We are the walking wounded. And we suffer alone because we don't know that there are others like us.[26]

The social mores that spill into private lives are a stark signpost to the structures that create and sustain mental ill health. Recognizing this helps explain how Styron (and others like him) can present their depression in terms of a humanist selfhood specifically *because* of the social space and capital he accrues as a privileged (and here, white) novelist. Because she is Black, Danquah is denied such security and community. The ghosts of her depression are interwoven with those built into her experiences of race.

In looking at work such as Danquah's, I find what I see as the fault lines and test limits of Medical Humanities and Disability Studies' status as disciplinary approaches, where the inevitable interweaving of life and health becomes a topic of critical enquiry. Such interweaving provokes an obvious question: why should we keep health and disability separate in ways that, as terms, Medical Humanities and Disability Studies clearly indicate? One answer is that, of course, this doesn't happen and that recognition of the overlappings of race, class, sexuality, gender, embodiment and others takes place all the time in intersectional work. But the disciplines' titles aren't meaningless, and the differing priorities and distinctions they create aren't simply products of academic legacies and institutional flag-waving.

Disciplinary differences themselves become constitutive of how health and disability become understood in the social imaginary. They funnel into media, for example, whether through journalism or the siren status of social media, and they inform political opinions. Medical Humanities and Disability Studies scholars are vehemently opposed to any allegations that their work is in any way part of an ivory-tower-research-for-its-own-sake paradigm (activism and teaching are prime examples of engaged commitment). Well, fine. But if that's so, we have to be attuned to how the critical parameters of our engaged work might inform debates surrounding health in ways that might actually be counterproductive.

Writing like Danquah's helps me make sense of this. In fact, in letting this book expand into the shape it needed to take, I found that it was writing by Black and other non-white authors that gave me crucial frames for my ideas. Because they are Black, Danquah and Ikpi provide complex interrogations of stigma not found in other life stories of mental ill health. They invoke the communal understandings of health I mentioned in the Introduction and as such are practitioners of the world naming I discuss above.[27] The fact that both are women was also a vital guide, allowing me to understand why a specific chapter on women's bodies would help me with my arguments, but also how gender is such a central marker of complexity in discussions of health and disability. As might be expected, there's a considerable amount of life writing by men that discusses ill health, but (as with Styron) it's often shaped by the power of the personal, a centrality that clusters around the individual expressed (obviously) in terms of patriarchal entitlement in one form or another. I read much of this but didn't find it useful in putting forward the arguments about Medical Humanities and Disability Studies that I found to be the most vital to address. Grue's book provided ideas that jumpstarted my thinking, but in what follows nearly all the figures on which I focus are women.[28] I have come to realize that the reason for this is simple: women's stories provide the best ways to analyse the disciplines because they are the most complex. They give the best critical insight into topics like disability/same and they do so with the kinds of indisciplined reasoning that signifies the most provocative (and therefore the most useful) modes of health telling.

Conclusion: Disciplines again

As a discipline, Medical Humanities is successful in many ways because it functions as a broad network of connected approaches across and through multiple subjects. It is through a synthesis of these, one imagined as much as actually theorized, that it lays claim to a critical power. In so doing, as a discipline it self-consciously *aspires* to greater sophistication; it has moved from deterministic models of instruction and listening (teaching doctors and consulting patients) to critical modes of entanglement and discipline crossing that ultimately are acts of complex *reading*.[29] Disability Studies *builds* sophistication into highly complex theoretical frames that host critical projects of advocacy and interrogations of social and cultural activities; it is wary of structures that discriminate and committed to the project of championing disabled presence and forms of knowing the world. In contrast, Medical Humanities still positions itself so as to carry the authority of the category of 'Medicine' (even as it critiques it) and, as a result, inevitably operates with some of the legitimacy the word accrues – I find this to especially be true at an institutional level. Through the use of a complex grid of enquiry it seeks to organize better, to challenge, and provide improved critical insight into how medicine and health work. Disability Studies is more interrogative of structures and the rethinking of space and time, more committed to activity and organized change. Because of its history as a subject that argues for the need to use the arts in health and to respect patients' voices, Medical Humanities still works through processes of *enlightenment*, an unveiling that demands more complexity as it asserts its place at the health and medicine table. In the ways in which Medical Humanities pushes to be more than a critical friend to clinical/academic conceptions of health, more than a recourse to humanist modes of understanding experience, for example, or a flat model of therapy, it has argued successfully – especially at levels of theory – for a need for interweaving, uncertainty and greater sophistication in seeing what health is. But arguably it does so through the *addition* of perspectives, even as its most critically complex. Disability Studies more fully names a recognizable and critical world, even in its sometimes contradictory and exasperated, forms.

At the same time, Medical Humanities aims for greater critical inclusivity and can push back against many of the uninterrogated assertions made by Disability Studies and the assumptions inherent in its affirmative modes of counter narratives. I have long found the argument that the 'medical model' of minds and bodies underpins misunderstanding of disabled bodies and minds to be frustrating (and this is even if such a model is not seen as that practised by medical specialists, but rather a public understanding of this practice). Do processes of medicine cause such problems because of their structures? Of course (think of the incredibly reductive nature of pain scales). Do they do so through recourse to an *overarching and coherent model* that guides this? Clearly not. Critical Disability thinking grounded in such a viewpoint can simplify the complexities of medicine and the arguments and tensions between different approaches to health and treatment: health-system officials insisting on discharging a patient from hospital, for example, set against rehabilitation experts who know that the person requires additional care; or a surgeon deeming an operation a success, when other doctors know complications are inevitable and they will have to deal with patient and family confusion about the future. I once heard a psychiatrist lament wearily that they felt the idea of a medical model was a construction by social scientists (especially) and cultural theorists that licensed dismissive straw-man arguments about medical practice, and I confess sympathy for that view. Disability Studies sometimes does the same with 'clinical' and 'biological' science (I have been guilty of the former). If critical work on disability can demand rightly that subtlety and nuance are essential to understanding its multiple manifestations, it's hardly reciprocal to resort to attacks on something called 'science' as a way of doing this.

In part, this problem arises because Disability Studies, understood here in its systemic disciplinary formations, isn't always good at being inclusive. Scholars in the separate subject areas that contribute to research on disability believe rightly that their work is often vital in addressing issues that affect the lives of disabled people. Working to reduce prejudice, institutional exclusion and systemic discrimination, or understanding cultural narratives, questions of representation and issues of gender (all 'for example's) is enough to take up the most of any working day and there isn't necessarily a need (or a desire) to attend to alternative ways of approaching disability experience. Many who work predominantly in Social Studies harbour suspicion towards the theoretical frameworks of Cultural Studies methods, while Critical Disability Studies may aim to build community, and so reaches out to engage with the thinking of others – gender/queer/race – because an alignment of methods can open new doors, but the results can be mixed. At its best and as I noted above, these processes are energizing, bringing rich discoveries to ongoing work. But they can be dismissive of research located in specific disciplinary approaches and also produce a lazy intersectionality that lines up critical approaches without thought and actually collapses the specificity of each. Similarly, a commitment to provocative engagement can assume that counter narratives to ableism are de facto good simply by existing in opposition. I often feel that the tendency of critical disability scholars to claim the moral high ground through an assertion of wide-ranging inclusion to be something that needs investigation and revision, because it all too often simplifies complexities of disability lives. I find more tolerance in Medical Humanities approaches to critical methods, possibly because the subject acknowledges that it doesn't have the same kind of foundational core subject (the disabled person, for example) as other disciplines. It knows that it needs to know more.

In much disability theory, assumptions are made about what disabled people *are* or what they *want* and even if these come within a language of inclusion that suggests variety, they can be remarkably inflexible (something I will discuss in later chapters). The sometime-stereotyping of the disabled person or consensus about what disability is and how it functions that is evident in much critical disability writing can be off-putting, especially when the desire is to champion the diversity of disabled lives. The settled agreement that results at times can easily become self-righteous.[30] A consensus needs to be challenged if it risks telling people how to think and what to do.

I'm aware that I've possibly been drawn into the position of choosing sides in the ways that I've structured the above, but I hope that it can be seen to be more than this. Putting different elements of the two disciplines in conversation and opposition is not about deciding that one is superior to the other; rather it admits that, like all critical approaches, they have strengths and weaknesses. In the two chapters that follow I want to play out all these thoughts. I'm an optimist, and as such I see them as provocative possibilities, ways of making interventions in the critical work that both Medical Humanities and Disability Studies undertake and therefore ways of better understanding medicine, health and disability across the wide range of their manifestations.

Notes

1. Anne Whitehead and Angela Woods, 'Introduction', in *The Edinburgh Companion to the Critical Medical Humanities* (Edinburgh: Edinburgh University Press, 2016), 2.

2. The Introduction to *Health Humanities Reader*, ed. Therese Jones, Delese Wear and Lester D. Friedman (New Brunswick, NJ, and London: Rutgers University Press, 2014), gives an excellent critical overview of the development of the discipline. See 'The Why, the What, and the How of the Medical/Health Humanities', n.p.

3. In *Bending Over Backwards*, Lennard J. Davis describes two instances where personal disability or disability studies was blocked from inclusion in a wider formation of multiculturalism because 'the issue of an identity defined by impairment as opposed to one defined by race or ethnicity' became what he terms a 'sticking point'. In the second example, where staff at Hunter College in New York City argued for disability studies to be made part of a multicultural curriculum, Davis notes that 'they were opposed by many of the ethnic and national groups that usually make up the progressive wing of the University' and that 'Hunter ended up deciding to omit disability from the curriculum'. Contemporary Disability Studies argues for the necessary value of a critical intersectionality, but it's worth remembering that such intersections have not always been possible. Lennard J. Davis, *Bending Over Backwards: Disability, Dismodernism, and Other Difficult Positions* (New York: New York University Press, 2002), 36–7.

4. See 'About Us', UCSF Medical Humanities. Available online: https://ucmedicalhumanitiespress.com/about-us/ (accessed 12 July 2002).

5. Whitehead and Woods, 'Introduction', 1.

6. I'm aware that, having just written an introduction focused on missing words, there's a phrase notable for its absence here in my discussion. In the US in particular, the expansion of Medical Humanities into new critical fields has created a new name for the discipline: Health Humanities. The division not only allows for the clear demarcation between the two approaches, but also designates what supporters of the new term see as a preferable model of inclusion. 'Medical' was understood to signal a problematic (over-)focus on doctors, a critical strategy that missed much of the way health actually manifests itself. 'Health' rectifies this, allowing for perspectives beyond those of doctors and medical researchers alone, a process that also creates greater critical diversity with more opportunities for, for example, approaches centred on gender. In the UK and other global locations, the change has not taken place for the most part (a fact that owes as much to the importance of funding schemes as any intellectual engagement) and what's understood as 'critical' Medical Humanities is now in effect the same as Health Humanities in the US.

My overwhelming response to this is one of frustration. It feels unnecessary to have separate labels for what are for the most part the same critical approaches, especially because of the subsequent energy wasted on discussions of the reasons. That frustration deepened as I realized that I was unable to get 'Health' into the title of this book: 'Medical/Health Humanities and Disability Studies: In/Disciplines' is just too garbled. But I take comfort from the fact that the series in which the book is placed *does* have the two terms together and would stress that I'm trying to write an intervention that works in terms of all the words found in both the series and individual book titles. Two additional thoughts: first, the considerable abiding strengths of the Medical Humanities model in the US, stressing pedagogy and Arts/Humanities approaches to the training of doctors and clinical practice, means that the label exists somewhat uneasily with the new 'Health' approach and it's noticeable that the contents of the influential 2014 collection *Health Humanities Reader* still contains both terms, sometimes used more or less interchangeably; my second observation is maybe more predictable – my own career to date has been explicitly within a Medical Humanities model, which I have always seen as multidisciplinary and complex enough to frame the arguments about health that I want to make.

7. I'm thinking here especially of the work of Dan Goodley and David Bolt in the UK. Goodley has written a series of expansive and insightful studies of the manifestations of disability across society and culture, the latest of which is *Disability and Other Human Questions* (Bingley: Emerald, 2021), for Emerald's SocietyNow series. In its format, SocietyNow is like this Provocation strand of Bloomsbury's Critical Interventions in the Medical and Health Humanities series, with short, ideas-led books designed for a wide audience. I feel a strong kinship with Goodley's work and see *Disability and Other Human Questions* as a kind of companion book to this one, with a similar commitment to stressing complexity but having its origins in a different critical point of view. Like Goodley, Bolt is based in a Department of Education, but has been the editor of the field-leading *Journal of Literary and Cultural Disability Studies* since its inception in 2008 and written on literary texts as well as education practice.

8. Lennard J. Davis, *Enforcing Normalcy: Disability, Deafness and the Body* (London and New York: Verso, 1995), 22. David Mitchell and Sharon Snyder's equally foundational critical study *Narrative Prosthesis: Disability and the Dependencies of Discourse* (Ann Arbor: The University of Michigan Press, 2000) works in a similar way.

9. Sharon L. Snyder and David T. Mitchell, *Cultural Locations of Disability* (Chicago: The University of Chicago Press, 2005).

10. Simi Linton, *Claiming Disability: Knowledge and Identity* (New York and London: New York University Press, 1998), 2.

11. Goodley puts this well, noting how Twitter is 'an echo chamber, an online primal scream therapy, a cacophony of voices, a mishmash of opinions or a digital shitstorm if you will' where users are 'in danger of being caught up for the killer one-liner, the likeable provocation, the retweetable-viewpoint-for-offensive-sake offering that increases online notoriety'. *Disability and Other Human Questions*, 124–5.

12. Davis, *Bending Over Backwards*, 13–14 and 22–3.

13. Michelle Friedner, *Valuing Deaf Worlds in Urban India* (New Brunswick, NJ: Rutgers University Press, 2015), 3.

14. In the conclusion to my 2008 book *Representing Autism: Culture, Narrative, Fascination* (Liverpool: Liverpool University Press), I wrote: 'Listening to those with autism has never been a more available option, and it is one that those who are in the business of making cultural representations of the condition need to take up' (212). Looking back, this seems unsophisticated and naive.

15. Slater, *Lying*, 221.

16. Bassey Ikpi, *I'm Telling The Truth But I'm Lying* (New York: HarperCollins, 2019), 49.

17. Meri Nana-Ama Danquah, *Willow Weep For Me: A Black Women's Journey through Depression* (New York and London: W. W. Norton, 1998), 20.

18. Danquah, *Willow Weep For Me,* 22 and 182.

19. William Styron, *Darkness Visible* (London: Vintage, 2004), 84.

20. Danquah, *Willow Weep For Me,* 103.

21. Ibid., 103–4.

22. Ibid., 108.

23. Ibid., 130 (italics in original).

24. Ibid., 104.

25. Danquah briefly mentions Styron in her memoir. When challenged by a newspaper editor to write an article on her depression because the success of *Darkness Visible* showed that there was 'a whole lot of stuff being written about depression these days', she counters: 'Like Styron and I would ever have the same angle on anything. We had the same illness, the similarities end there. The way I did depression was a-whole-nother bag of beans. I'm a single black mother about half a paycheck away from the government cheeseline.' Danquah, *Willow Weep For Me,* 235.

26. Ibid., 184.

27. I really wanted to include in this section a discussion of Michael Dorris's book *The Broken Cord*, published in 1989. Dorris's memoir deals with the adoption of his son Adam (real name Reynold Abel), who had Fetal Alcohol Spectrum Disorder, and spirals out into so many other complexities. It cover processes of adoption within Native American communities, the associated ethics of parental responsibility, and the prejudice and stigma this involves (personal and historical, particularly when discussing the prevalence of FASD and paucity of healthcare in First Nations communities in the US). In its engagement with these topics, it exemplifies what I want to showcase as community approaches to health that move beyond the personal and the way in which Dorris firmly situates how he raised his son within tribal and cross-tribal dynamics is central to the story. *The Broken Cord* was celebrated, winning various national awards, and brought Dorris fame, respect and status, but its legacy took a turn following post-publication events: Adam was killed in a car accident as a teenager; two of Dorris's other children accused him of sexual assault; and he subsequently committed suicide in 1997. The link between these last two events remains contested. An initial article on Dorris in *New York* magazine that contained the allegations of abuse was shown by a subsequent piece in the *Washington Post* to have contained numerous inaccuracies, though the status of this second article has to be read within the complex dynamics of claims and counter claim. As both memoir and the prompt for the cascade of incidents that followed it, *The Broken Cord* signals as complex a set of health-connected topics as I can

imagine. It is a perfect example of the idea of text as exemplar of the case limit of Medical Humanities and Disability Studies. But it also became a limit of my ability to write on disability and health. I simply couldn't cover everything it dealt with. Dorris, *The Broken Cord* (New York: Harper & Row, 1989).

28. Filmmaker Jonathan Caouette, discussed in the next chapter, is one exception, although Caouette's queerness is central to his film. I'm aware that the major male figure who provides source material for the book is me.

29. I'm grateful to Amelia DeFalco for the insight about reading. It's true – Medical Humanities is such a reading-focused discipline, whatever its subject area. Reading and interpreting drive much of its work. Across the full range of Disability Studies, activity is far more important,

30. It's anecdotal, but disability critic Robert McRuer once said, with some exasperation, that there need to be more arguments in the discipline. And in *Crip Theory* he distinguished between Crip and Disability Studies approaches to their topics, asserting that 'crip theory is more contestatory than disabilities studies'. Robert McRuer, *Crip Theory: Cultural Signs of Queerness and Disability* (New York: New York University Press, 2006), 35.

REFLECTION 2: SUNDAY IN THE PARK WITH LUCAS

There are consequences to being late, so I break from a fast walk into an inelegant trot/run as I try to make up time. It's Sunday morning and I need to get to the local park where my son Lucas will be dropped off for what is has been our weekly catch-up since he moved into new assisted accommodation. Except it hasn't been weekly for over a year. For much of 2020, I've been unable to see Lucas. The Covid lockdown rules for his home have made visits impossible and he hasn't had even the limited opportunities to be outside that the rest of his family have managed. While I'm worried about being late and causing him to be frustrated, a larger part of my anxiety is simply the overwhelming nature of everything the last few months have been. I have no idea of how this will go. In truth, I can't even properly register how I feel. Being late doesn't help.

This is the second time I have seen him since he has been allowed to leave his home. The first was the briefest of walks months ago, just before a second lockdown. Rather than anything we did, my memory of that day is more of the incredible surprise on his face when he saw me – a burst of recollection, seeing someone who (this was my reading of it) he might have thought he was never going to see again. I was a mess as I took his hand, trying to hold things together and talk to the staff who had driven him here. Today, he is surprised again, though on this occasion the first thing I note is that he is paler than usual because of being inside for so long. He hums, an indeterminate sound that I cannot read – happy, confused, somewhere inbetween? I usually have a feel for his various noises and am worried that I've forgotten what they signify.

Lucas is twenty-one. He was a wiry, thin child, mainly because of a chronically poor diet. Once, during a clear-out at home, I found a food diary I kept for him when on holiday in 2003. According to my notes, he ate two bowls of pasta, some yogurts, crisps and a few apples over a two-week period. Now he eats better and has developed into a tall young man, broad shouldered and with a strong back. His short hair is dark black. His gaze flits, rarely focusing on my face. I have always felt that he looks at me just enough to know what he feels he *needs to, an efficient check-in to gauge what I'm saying or might be asking him to do.*

We have a usual route round the park. Lucas runs to the side of a small children's play area where he sits down on his haunches and rubs the palms of his hands over his ears. He does this a lot, to the extent that some of the hair just above his ears has worn away. He is still humming. As always, I wait for him to get up, something that can take any amount of time. I talk to him, tell him about the rest of us, the people who know and love him. I wasn't sure how I would feel as I set off to meet him, and trying to express this in words I realize that I'm self-conscious and making little sense. He gets up and we walk round a large pond, a route covered in the goose shit that gives the park a notoriety. Lucas has bright white trainers on, a pair he has had for several years and that (it has occurred to me) are possibly now desirable in a retro fashion kind of way. I've always liked an element of dressing him in ways that might not be expected; I bought him a too-big Harvard Business School hoodie when he was about eight, to grow into, and enjoyed the idea of people meeting him having to confront a clearly autistic boy with words emblazoned across his chest that signalled the epitome of successful economic credentials. It was – I admit – a kind of fuck-you to everyone else, and clearly more about me than him. Now, however, we're just in the business of avoiding the geese and keeping the trainers clean.

We're heading for the park café. He hasn't forgotten the way – he never would – and so far everything has gone okay. We walk under willow trees that bend to the pond, ducking their trailing branches. The café has been open a few weeks and we're going to be able to sit outside on its terrace. He will have orange juice and a pack of salt and vinegar crisps, I'll have a coffee and we'll sit together. It's what we do. As we approach the door, I realize that I'm seriously on edge. If there's any difference inside the café, any change of layout or what's on offer, there will be no way to explain to him why. If he's upset, he might push against me, against the door, or could sit down and refuse to move. He's done this before. For me, these kinds of moments, crossing thresholds, are often the most distressing and stressful.

I'm relieved that the café seems to be completely the same. It's not busy and there's no queue, but like everyone I have a continual reminder of the danger of proximity, a low-level anxiety that feels imprecise but nevertheless palpable. In addition, last time we were in the café – many months ago – Lucas had a completely unpredictable outburst, a sudden physical explosion in which he *leapt from his chair and ran across the room, coming close to knocking over two small children and nearly making the door before I caught up with him. That shook me, not only because it came from nowhere, but also because it was a reminder of when he was younger and this kind of event was common. I am worried about him doing the same now.*

I find a table on the terrace close to the open door and Lucas sits, but I'm still nervous. I have to go inside to the counter to collect our drinks and worry that he will run in the ten or so seconds I am away. I walk up in a strange half-turned position, overthinking everything, too much information and too much processing to do. I get back to our table, but that doesn't lessen my anxiety. A history is in play here and I'm being reminded too much of the past. It is a bright day in late summer, it's wonderful to be able to see my son again, but none of that is making any difference.

When we sit, my whole body is tuned to the possibility of problem and even conflict, simply by being here. Because of previous experiences when out with Lucas in public, I feel that everyone watching is intolerant, potentially a bigot. They're prejudiced and don't understand autism or disability. Lucas is loud, as he often is, a mini-symphony of rising and falling sounds. Now that I'm tuning in, I can tell that today's noises are poised somewhere between contentment and frustration, none of the high notes of outright happiness. Inevitably, people are staring. I react by grabbing his iPad, selecting the 'About Me' tab on his communication software, and pressing on the 'My name is Lucas' symbol. It is voiced out loud, loud enough for those on the tables closest to hear. I press on it five times in a row: 'My name is Lucas.' 'My name is Lucas.' 'My name is Lucas.' 'My name is Lucas.' 'My name is Lucas.' To me, this is a statement of his presence, of his right to be here, in his way on his terms. It's a rebuke to those who think he's different, a push-back to their inherent ableism and limited view of the world, a demand to respect his selfhood.

It's nothing of the sort, of course. Lucas isn't saying this – I am. I'm not only ventriloquizing but, worse, appropriating his right to say his own name. It's me, and not him, who's having a sensory overload, me who's overwhelmed by the environment. I'm the one who would like to curl up and be elsewhere.

This is a disability same moment, except here everyone other than me is the same. Lucas is the same and does not seem to be especially disturbed by all the things I have brought to the situation. And the people in the café are the same – there's no evidence that any of them are prejudiced or ignorant; they're going about their Sundays. There's simply me, raging with an unstitched, unravelling patchwork of worry. The worst thing about it, I realize, is that I've turned the moment into a Disability Studies 101 seminar – the oppressive nature of normalcy, an ableist negation of difference – and it's nothing like that at all. It's just me being late and feeling guilty and stressed, forgetting things, or doing them wrong. My knowledge of disability isn't helping me at all here; it's doing exactly the opposite. There could be people here with more knowledge of disability, even of autism, than I have. People who have disabilities in their own families, or work with a disability organization maybe, or have disabilities of their own that I can't see. And even if there aren't these, there are probably people who care, who feel emotional as they watch, who are supportive. There could be people here absolutely loving that post-lockdown a man is able to go outside with his disabled son.

I've seen this version of myself in other parents and carers; at visitor attractions on a sunny day in the school holidays, or by the edge of a crowded and noisy swimming pool in winter. The hypervigilance, the awareness that something could go wrong any second. The sheer anxiety of it all. And it's not wrong to feel that, because sometimes it does go wrong. But today I'm the one being judgemental, anticipating what others are like, stereotyping strangers and projecting feelings onto them.

We leave. Covid protocols mean that we have to exit and walk round the building the opposite way we entered. This IS different, and I need to explain and nudge/push Lucas, my shoulder to his, so we go the right way. It works and we're – literally – back on course. I'm coming down from the paranoia, but I realize that the worst thing is that I haven't done what I wanted to the most – enjoy the time together. Our walk takes us past empty tennis courts and round the end of the pond, back past a small open theatre space where amateur productions sometimes take place and a basketball court where a teenager with a serious stare hits free throws. I know that it's strange to see two grown men with such an obvious age difference holding hands, especially from a distance. Maybe it makes more sense when we get closer.

When I worked a lot on autism in the first decade of this century, there were often vicious discussions in the community about the respective positions of parents of autistic children and autistic adults. The adult activists saw parents as figures who wanted to somehow find the child they thought they had lost, and who sought out medical or therapeutic practices that would drag their sons and daughters out of the shell in which they felt autism trapped them. To want this, the activists asserted, was to want a different person and to hate the child you have, even to want them dead. I never felt this, never wanted Lucas to be anyone other than he was, but I remember the hostility of the arguments as I argued such a position, personally and in writing. Part of my response was a complex, if inevitable, over-complication; an often-ferocious commitment to the rights of the disabled person thoroughly interwoven with the worry and sheer exhaustion that came with being a parent. Any parent will tell you that having children takes you to your limits and shows you what is beyond your control; being the parent of a disabled child is this multiplied, I found, especially when you think about a future after you have gone.

And this is disability same as well. That day, I realized, it wasn't only the overcrowded emotions of the café, it was the latest iteration of feelings that had been there since those first moments as a toddler when Lucas stopped making eye contact. Even after all this time apart – the longest I'd gone without seeing him in his life – that worry and fear revealed itself to be nothing new. And despite the fact that I'd felt it for nearly twenty years, I'd misunderstood it again.

We take a turn down to the river. I had tried to lengthen our walk on one occasion by including more of the river path but he was having none of it, that day or since. He knows exactly where the car park is. The driver gets out of the car and we talk about how things have gone. He takes a photo of us and I persuade Lucas to give me a head bump that is our substitute for a kiss, though I then kiss him anyway. He gets in the car and I shut the door and tap on the window. He flits me a look, just a little check, and then the car drives away.

I walk home, slowly. Overall, maybe it had gone okay. The thing that counts, I tell myself, is that Lucas enjoyed it. That's both maybe true – if I'm honest, I couldn't tell – and a clear denial, because my version of the event is obviously important. As I'm processing this I reflect on one thought, though, that we'll be able to do it all again next weekend, the whole thing once more: same time, same place, with whatever difference comes with it.

CHAPTER 2
MEDICINE/HEALTH/
DISABILITY/MINDS

States of meds

There's a blink-and-you'll-miss-it moment about mental health and medication in Ron Howard's 2001 film *A Beautiful Mind*, his biopic of mathematician John Nash. Nash, whose schizophrenia affected much of his adult life, has outlined in interviews how he stopped taking medication altogether in the early 1970s because of a worry that it inhibited his thinking (and that in fact he was very selective in his medication use before this date). This detail is perfect material for Howard's narrative, which seeks to chart Nash's journey from precocious young genius to Nobel laureate, passing through the demons of mental ill health on the way. As opposed to portraying a health condition regulated by medicine, *A Beautiful Mind* asks its audience to see Nash's life as an individualistic struggle, abetted by the love and understanding of family and friends but ultimately driven by willpower, to conquer the terrifying delusions of his altered state. Nash's award of the 1994 Nobel Memorial Prize in Economic Sciences is, the film suggests, a fitting reward for the actual beauty of his mind, one which was battered by schizophrenia but endured to be recognized for its brilliance by the highest authority in academia.[1]

The moment itself is throwaway (when I teach the film, a majority of the students don't pick up on it) and comes near the end, following Nash's rehabilitation after his institutionalization. As an aside, Nash mentions in conversation – in a mumble that's barely more than a whisper – that he's taking 'some of the newer medication'. The film's narrative around medication up to this point has stressed Nash's rejection of pharmaceutical intervention; he is seen putting pills in a box as opposed to taking them and articulates that 'being crazy' is better than losing the critical faculties that make his research possible. Medicine, it's clear, stops him from being himself. The reference to newer medication disappears as soon as it arrives, however, with a quick return to the story's emphasis on self-discipline and resolve, and the need to literally 'look away' from the hallucinations and delusions (represented in the film as real characters) that plague him. Being on medication of any kind, then, clearly makes no sense; it's a flat contradiction of a central element of what the film creates as Nash's trajectory through his illness. But of course the production team realized exactly why the line needs to be there: a high-profile A-list Hollywood production focusing on schizophrenia can't advocate that those with the condition don't take medication. The real Nash recognized this, saying in a Nobel interview that 'the director in the movie didn't want to suggest that people who are living with controlled mental illness – that they should stop taking their medicine. It would be dangerous to suggest this'.[2] But *A Beautiful Mind* precisely *is* a film that does this. Rejecting medication is part of what makes Nash's mind 'beautiful'. Actual medical practice might have to be acknowledged but can't get in the way of a foundational arc of the life-affirming story. A barely noticeable whisper will do.

I stress this moment because for me it's a particular version of the kinds of narrative that swirl around the purported understanding of mental illness. It is so clearly nonsensical that it goes beyond the messy contradictions that usually cluster around depictions of health (in my less articulate moments I have called it 'mad'). Why this is the case is, of course, primarily to do with the juggernaut that is the world's most influential film industry, where such blatant disregard of coherence is standard. But it is more than this. It is made possible by the desire and fear that are prompted by, here, schizophrenia, the push and pull that come when the visceral matter of such conditions is faced. It was Aristotle who claimed that man is a rational animal, instituting a foundational tradition of seeing the idea of reason in person-centred terms. The fear of madness is that, in the title of Elyn Saks' memoir that I will discuss later, this 'center (sic) cannot hold'. In Sander Gilman's words, 'the most elementally frightening possibility' of a condition like schizophrenia 'is loss of control over the self, and loss of control is associated with loss of language and thought perhaps even more than with physical illness'. As an 'antithesis to the control and reason that define the self', mental ill health, Gilman notes, appears to threaten the very core of what constitutes human presence.[3] The fear is that being inchoate is the norm and the lack of balance in 'being unbalanced' or the absence of quantifiable measure in 'being unsound' are persistent and systemic. 'Uncontrollable' becomes double in this paradigm of fear; it is both the lack of any individual ability to control oneself, and the associated impossibility of controlling the person who is mad.

Say it out loud

The mumble in Howard's film invites an investigation into how critical discourses of medicine and disability vary and clash in their approaches to mental illness. Just as the inconsistency in *A Beautiful Mind* creates a fissure in the film's logic, a crack that widens the more it's thought through, these approaches work with unease around the subject matter of (broadly conceived) cognitive difference and/or illness. More often than not, clinical medicine focuses on mental ill health as a pathology and seeks alleviation and cure as attempts to restore equilibrium, but this has always been contested. From the work of Thomas Szasz, R.D. Laing and others during the anti-psychiatry movements of the 1960s and 1970s onwards, an element of mental health research has queried the efficacy of treatment based around such a model of pathology, choosing to give greater emphasis to context (Laing's argument that insanity is a perfectly rational adjustment to an insane world is possibly the most famous example of this). Committed to this emphasis on the disabling effects of context, Disability Studies has a longstanding suspicion of cure, seeing it as driven by social norms that coalesce around what becomes formed as the 'acceptable' body or mind. Cure is understood here as a potential vehicle for erasure and the eradication of all that is seen as threatening to a non-ill majority. As the social model of disability developed from the 1970s onwards, a nascent 'Mad Movement' ran alongside it, with a lower profile but similar positioning. The advent of the contemporary Mad Studies discipline owes much to the organising, activism and performances of this previous generation and the ways it pushed back against the suppositions of mental coherence central to the clinical encounter.

This chapter will focus on schizophrenia in its exploration of the tensions that exist between Disability Studies and Medical Humanities approaches to mental illness. Schizophrenia appears as the *sine qua non* of altered cognition, the most expressive – and therefore most frightening – form of mental illness. It is the essence of craziness, of lunacy. As a label, it signifies a terrifying rupture, the very sound of the name carrying connotations of that lack of control cited by Gilman. The word itself is powerful: 'Say the word "schizophrenia" out loud a few times', Nathan Filer writes in his book on the condition. 'Say it loud enough that you feel self-conscious; that you worry someone will hear. Say it loud enough that someone might hear. Feel the shape of it. Stay with it. Think about what that word evokes in you. What thoughts does it arrive with? What feelings?' As he goes on to note, 'whole lives have disappeared beneath' it.[4] In *Girl, Interrupted*, one of the most well-known memoirs outlining the experience of mental ill health, Susanna Kaysen asks: 'and what about schizophrenia – that would send a chill up your spine. That's real insanity. After all, people don't "recover" from schizophrenia.'[5] In *Far From the Tree: Parents, Children and the Search for Identity*, Andrew Solomon calls the illness one of 'replacement and deletion', a disease that 'eliminates' the person that has it.[6] For Lauren Slater, the chronically schizophrenic patients she worked with at the start of her career as a therapist appeared as 'the grotesques of this world, burdened by the most horrifying psychiatric illness known to mankind'.[7] In *Welcome To My Country*, her memoir of this work, Slater quotes the start of a 1985 editorial in the *Australian and New Zealand Journal of Psychiatry*, entitled 'The Costs of Schizophrenia' that states flatly: 'Schizophrenia is to psychiatry what cancer is to general medicine: a sentence as well as a diagnosis.'[8] In *Mental Traveler*, his book about his son Gabe's schizophrenia, academic W.J.T. Mitchell also makes the link to cancer, calling the condition a 'death sentence' that 'produces a shudder'. Mitchell also notes that he 'hated schizophrenia for what it was doing to my son. I sometime regarded it as a demon that needed to be exorcized, and indeed, it sometimes did feel like a form of alien presence.'[9] The list could go on, but the point is possibly made best in the very opening line of Esmé Weijun Wang's book of essays, *The Collected Schizophrenias*: 'Schizophrenia terrifies.'[10]

Is there a mental health condition more *medical* than schizophrenia? It appears to signal endlessly its medicalized status. Heavyweight academic journals (*Schizophrenia Bulletin, Schizophrenia Research, npj Schizophrenia*) publish a non-stop flow of new research on the condition, while huge conferences organized by international associations such as the Schizophrenia International Research Society bring together scholars and clinicians from all over the world to discuss every imaginable aspect of its manifestations.[11] The word interweaves with others – schizoaffective, psychosis, schizotypy, dysphoria, mania, psychopathology, just to name a few[12] – that are equally saturated with medical inflection. Schizophrenia's medical state confirms and underscores its apparent unknowability; if it weren't so terrifyingly impenetrable, it wouldn't need *so much* medicine.

For all of its seemingly inherent wildness, it's important to stress here the ways in which all understandings of schizophrenia, as with mental health more widely, belong in context – indeed are often created by context. Whatever the latest best practice, whether through talking therapy or advances in understanding neurology, the terms of treatment always expose the apparatus of their construction. In *The Protest Psychosis: How Schizophrenia Became a Black Disease*, Jonathan Metzl pinpoints how in the US in the 1960s the condition became what he terms a racialized disease, in which African American men were labelled schizophrenic because of the contextual ways in which, overdetermined as 'black [sic] men', they came to be understood (especially in terms of perceived aggression and violence). He observes: 'At the end of the day, the fact that these men became schizophrenic had relatively little to do with the men's actions [but was rather] because of changes of interpretive structures surrounding their actions.' African American men developed schizophrenia 'not because of changes in their clinical presentation, but because of changes in the connections between their clinical presentation and larger, national conversations and race, violence, and insanity'. As with Meri Nana-Ama Danquah's understanding of her depression explored in the Introduction, schizophrenia here isn't about symptoms; it's about racism. And again as with Danquah's recognition of the connections between such perspectives and gender, this racism spread from models of evaluating mental health to include conceptions of masculinity, as well as the development of pharmaceutical treatments, and the very idea of 'character': a specific twentieth-century medical version of centuries-old discourses of prejudice and discrimination. As Metzl notes, in the 1960s to *be* schizophrenic increasingly meant to be a black man.[13]

It is important, if predictable and highly discouraging, to note that such inequalities are perpetuated. A 2021 study of the ways in which people with psychosis in the UK's Black Caribbean population navigate the country's mental health system confirmed that, as has been the case for forty years, in the present 'persistent inequalities exist in how individuals from minority ethnic groups access mental health care, highlighting higher rates of compulsory admission to psychiatric hospitals, and the increased involvement of police, among black Caribbean people with psychosis compared with the white British population'. The authors concluded: 'The data suggests that distress among black and minority ethnic groups is rooted in social structures that disadvantage black (sic) people. Black participants appeared most vulnerable to oppressive master narratives and most likely to experience psychiatry as another form of oppression that did not address the sources of their distress.'[14] While this study notes inequality, oppression and distress, there is equally an increasing trend to see people with mental illness as dangerous, especially as potential perpetrators of violence. That this becomes explicitly racialized is inevitable when systems of assessment and treatment characterize and discriminate in the ways made clear here.

The idea of *becoming* schizophrenic, then, is wide-ranging. The above examples highlight race and gender, but their processes equally manifest through interactions with sexuality, disability and cultural difference to produce similar effects. The perceived threat attached to people with schizophrenia is that they are uncontained and that their condition might manifest itself in the open and without control. One consequence of this is an interweaving of medical and legal approaches that come together to stress a need for confinement, the 'compulsory admission' in the above UK example. It is this social and institutional need that Wang faced when, on three occasions between 2002 and 2011, she was hospitalized against her will. Her memory of it is vivid:

It is hard to convey the horror of being involuntarily committed. First, there's the terrifying experience of forcibly being put in a small place from which you're not allowed to leave. You're also not allowed to know how long you'll be there, because no one knows how long you'll be there. You don't have the things you love with you: your journal, the bracelet your grandmother gave you, your favourite socks. Your teddy bear [...] A lot of the time, your possessions won't be permitted into the ward because they include a sharp point or a wire coil or a dangerous piece of cloth. You're not allowed to choose what you eat, and within the limited choices that do exist, you're forced to choose between things that are disgusting. You are told when to sleep and when to wake up.[15]

The processes of committal, she observes, mean that although 'Humans might be all ciphers to one another', it's people with mental illness who are deemed 'particularly opaque because of their broken brains. We cannot be trusted about anything, including our own experiences'.[16] For those, like Wang, subjected to this form of restraint, it is not an outside perception of threat – to herself or others – that dominates her recollection of events. Rather it is the complexity of what was taken from her.

In writing this chapter, I read across multiple national Mental Healthcare Acts – from Europe, Africa and Asia – to see how they each articulate their processes for involuntary confinement. For all their specifics and difference, the words and ideas the Acts contain – compulsory, committed, withdrawn, restricted, forcible, removed, sequestered, sectioned, detained, involuntary, subject to warrant – are remarkably similar. Without exception they create the parameters that shaped Wang's experience and given the substantial cultural differences between the various countries, the uniformity of the language is striking. Each of the Acts makes clear statements about the need to respect the privacy and dignity of those being detained, and that such measures are operated only as a last resort, but there is a pronouncement of authority inherent in their prose that is inevitably part of the kinds of national and geocultural conditions of evaluating mental health Metzl sees as being central to the structural control inherent in such judgement. I can't imagine a scenario where it would not be appropriate, because of specific certain circumstances, for some people to be detained against their will, but detainment often becomes forced coercion and treatment, with assumptions made about what constitutes individual best interests. Clearly, such processes can be highly traumatic for the people subject to their terms, but they also become part of the very fabric by which mental illness becomes created and understood, both at an institutional level and in terms of public perception.

Writing excess

Schizophrenia threatens narrative (of all kinds) because of its suggestion of chaos, its sheer unpredictability and commitment to damaging excess. At the same time, as Wang notes: 'The story of schizophrenia is one with a protagonist, "the schizophrenic"'. This protagonist has no real corollary in other mental health conditions, no similar central naming of a subject (possibly 'the depressive' once performed a similar function, but it is antiquated and now rarely used), and the effect of the suggested chaos is heightened because the threat has a figure to which to attach. Wang observes that 'the schizophrenic' 'is first a fine and good vessel with fine and good things inside of it, and then becomes misshapen through the ravages of psychosis [...] Finally, the wicked thoughts and behaviour become inseparable from the person, who is now unrecognizable from what they once were.'[17] All these ideas of attack, destruction and eradication are played out in the ways in which the dark tumultuous energy of schizophrenia annihilates and obliterates those who have the condition.

Most memoirs written on the experience of schizophrenia stress these elements and the challenge they pose to ideas to selfhood, with a particular emphasis on the possibility of finding a pathway through the illness.[18] Saks' book is probably the best known, recounting what she calls her 'journey through madness' (the subtitle of *The Center Cannot Hold*). A common feature of schizophrenia writing is the difficulty in describing the impediments to such a journey, whether these are personal or through structures of healthcare, and for all that the condition might seem so unrelentingly medical, reading these stories is to see time and again how the language and practice of medicine fails to match the way the illness manifests itself. It requires more than the flat terms that open the *DSM-5* definition: delusions, hallucinations, disorganized speech, grossly disorganized/catatonic behaviour, negative symptoms (I know that this last is using 'negative' in a specific clinical manner, but have always felt that it reads as a kind of giving up on an attempt to describe, a term so bland it feels like an admission of the impossibility of naming). Wang says that reading the *DSM* definition of her experience was 'to be cast far from the horror of psychosis and an unbridled mood; it shrink-wraps the bloody circumstance with objectivity until the words are colorless'.[19]

Making the 'colorless' bloody, reclaiming it for what it is, is a challenge for both those who choose to write their personal histories and the academic disciplines, whether Medical Humanities, Disability Studies or others, that want to address these. It asks for a creative hermeneutics that can at least try to say what schizophrenia feels like. It might speak through metaphors, parallels, emotions, make aesthetics and shake up the temporal and the visual. For Saks, explaining the experience is 'much harder, and weirder, to describe than extreme fear or terror'. She continues:

> The 'me' becomes a haze, and the solid center from which one experiences reality breaks up like a bad radio signal. There is no longer a sturdy vantage point from which to look at, take things in, assess what's happening. No core holds things together, providing the lens through which to see the world, to make judgements and comprehend risk. Random moments of time follow one another. Sights, sounds, thoughts, and feelings don't go together. No organizing principle takes successive moments in time and puts them together in a coherent way from which sense can be made. And it's all taking place in slow motion.[20]

This really is an extraordinary passage. The feelings and impressions Saks experiences are scattered and need metaphors – haze, radio signals, lenses – while time and image are slowed down and made random. But the desire for a recognizable and contained 'me' is so powerful: see how centre, reality, sturdy, core, judgment, comprehension, organizing, and coherence are all working. As a high-achieving medical student training to be a clinician, Saks craves the rational even as her life gives her screams, conspiracies, and disembodied voices that make up the full palette of psychosis. She never fully lets go of the Cartesian split that allows her to pride herself on her mind – her academic brilliance, the ability to think things through. 'For years, I'd seen my body as the place that I lived, and the real me was in my mind', she observes near the end of her book; 'the body was just the carrying case, and not a very dependable one – kind of dirty, animal-like, unreliable.' And although she says that this has decreased as she has grown older – 'I'm more comfortable with my body lately; maybe even more possessive of it' – she is 'wary at the same time'. It is her body that 'let me down more than a few times'.[21]

It's fitting, then, that Saks talks of schizophrenia in terms of it being a haze or fog – 'Schizophrenia rolls in like a slow fog, becoming imperceptibly thicker as time goes on' – because the effect of fog is precisely to impede, but not destroy, clarity; to impair what she calls the lens that allows her to see the world.[22] The metaphor of a descending fog is common in memoirs of schizophrenia. In *A Road Back from Schizophrenia* (more travelling), Arnhild Lauveng begins her story with the gradual onset of a fog that 'slowly creeps over the sky'. When she started to realize this, that the sun has stopped shining and the birds were no longer singing, it is too late: 'by then the fog is already there, the sun is gone, landmarks are starting to disappear, and you don't have time to find your way home because the fog is so heavy that all the roads are gone.'[23] Lauveng has dramatic hallucinations – she is one of the few schizophrenics who has extreme vivid visual experiences, seeing people, dragons that swallow princesses, large rats attacking her as she cycles home from school, Dali-esque bending of streets and houses as she walks – but she begins her memoir with fog, the haze that masks the real. Giant rats are simply madness; but fog can clear.

It is no coincidence that both Saks and Lauveng are clinicians: Saks a Professor of Law, Psychology, and Psychiatry and the Behavioral Sciences, expert on mental health law and influential member of the schizophrenia research community; Lauveng a clinical psychologist working in Norway. For each, medical science has provided a route out of chaos. Lauveng tells us that she knows 'how it feels to be handcuffed in the back of a car or how wallpaper tastes' but that she is 'healthy' and 'well' (indeed she goes so far as to call herself a 'former schizophrenic', even though she acknowledges that this 'basically doesn't exist. It is a role that is never offered').[24] Saks has a career that, in and of itself, marks her as extraordinary; it is a journey that seems impossible because of her health. She is more cautious than Lauveng in her assessment of the personal nature of the pathway she has taken, however. 'My good fortune is not that I've recovered from mental illness. I have not, nor will I ever', she writes, 'My good fortune lies in having found my life'.[25] Though both writers differ on where they have found themselves, they have clarity in common: the centre *does* hold ('found my life') and the road back can be taken. The fog has been made to lift.

There is a power to these stories. They don't deny the visceral reality of schizophrenia and find metaphors that enable the telling of the craziness, but they show how it can be faced. It is writing that wins awards, gets taught, finds audiences and does work in the world. My copy of *The Center Cannot Hold* has an interview with Saks and reading group guide at the end ('What did you learn'? 'Did it change your perspective in any way?' 'If you've dealt with chronic illness, how is the author's experience the same or different than your experience'? 'How is your mind your worst enemy and best friend?')[26] But as I read through Saks' and Lauveng's stories of finding their way through impediments, I kept thinking of the dragons and the rats, the slow motion and randomness, the bloody, that which happens when the fog is stubborn and refuses to leave. What anyone might learn from the apparition of a princess-eating dragon is maybe a challenge to articulate and how it might differ from your experience as a member of a reading group is a tricky question to answer. I could well be in a minority, but that's a conversation I would like to have.

In doing this, there's a need to find the right critical language. Saks and Lauveng (and many others like them) are the kinds of 'voices' honoured in the practice of narrative medicine and that branch of the Medical Humanities that sees how life stories are educational and instructive, for both the public and training clinicians. As such, they are all participants in what becomes a process of looping: a medical condition that becomes written retrospectively by a medical specialist, read in medical contexts (and I include public appreciation in this) and then given a home within medical practice and academic disciplines that want to tell as many experiences of health as possible so as to better know its subjects. I can feel this paragraph drifting towards cynicism and need to push back against that. I don't see how undergraduate students with schizophrenia taking part in the kind of conference on mental illness and academia that Saks organized in 2014 is anything other than wonderful, for example. Maybe there was room for discussing dragons. But I want an approach that can talk about these things in another way, to focus (as with so much of this book) on what's missing. I can't help but feel dissatisfied with how meaning is attributed to these stories, how the voices are made to sound similar. This is random I know, and possibly unfair, but at the time of writing this sentence (February 2022) the latest 'First Person Account' in the most recent issue of *Schizophrenia Bulletin* (such accounts appear in each issue) is by a scientist who focuses on the efficacy of various medicines in treating their psychosis across an academic career and concludes that 'It is very useful for clinicians to understand the behaviors of the patients and for academics to get insights about psychosis in schizophrenia'. These behaviours are, it's made clear, a set of 'puzzles' that can be explained through such insight.[27]

The critical resources I found myself drawn to as I started to think more about schizophrenia were those that didn't seek to explain puzzles. The first of these were the memoirs themselves. I have always believed that the best creative and life-writing texts are theory, that they practice criticism. There is no critical discussion of *Girl, Interrupted* and mental illness that is anywhere near as sophisticated and insightful on the topic as Kaysen's memoir itself, for example. Its jagged structure, provocations, careful plotting, knowing tone and (dis)honesty are an extraordinary set of narrative and theoretical effects that tell truths not found in the critical writing. With schizophrenia, I gravitated towards certain writers, filmmakers and artists who I feel do similar things. Beyond this, I saw a need to understand the excessive, chaotic nature of the condition as best framed by critical thinking that comes from Disability Studies: Alison Kafer's and Ellen Samuels' ideas of crip time for the too slow/too fast temporality of psychosis; Tobin Siebers' complex embodiment or David Mitchell's and Sharon Snyder's biopolitics and disability matter/affect for the physical manifestations of the illness; and the disability-inflected and survivor-led Mad Studies movement for the social presence of resisting the juggernaut of what Peter Beresford has termed the 'western psych-system' that 'has been exported and imposed wholesale' on the remainder of the globe.[28]

This last point is important. As Beresford notes, Mad Studies has been criticized – for being elitist, lacking inclusivity, and using language that many survivors find problematic – but he defends it as 'the first survivor-led movement' addressing mental ill health 'that has sought to develop a strong philosophical and theoretical base'. The inspiration for this, he makes clear, is the disabled people's movement that, from its beginning, focused on 'philosophy and theory as a basis for thought and action'.[29] Madness then, that most medical of subjects, is here reworked, resisted and claimed in a critical Disability, and not Medical Humanities, frame. The life narratives invite these disability readings: Saks' slow motion is an overt reference to the ways in which schizophrenia profoundly disturbs time, but it is exactly the kind of 'challenge to normative and normalizing expectations of pace and scheduling' that Kafer sees as a central component of crip time. 'Rather than bend bodies and minds to meet the clock', she adds, 'crip time bends the clock to meet disabled bodies and minds'.[30] It is the world of the crip that provides the terms to understand the bending inherent in schizophrenia and found so frequently in memoirs of the condition.

Thinking about bending takes me back to Jan Grue's body and the stories he tells with it in *I Live a Life Like Yours*, a memoir that is firmly disabled. Understanding schizophrenia through disability frees up opportunities to see not only the condition's agile kinks and twists, but the off-centre ways in which those who experience schizophrenia tell their tales. Wang describes the complex positioning of her subjectivity in exactly these terms, and in ways that offer a clear parallel to Grue. Describing a talk on her schizophrenia she gave at a health clinic in San Francisco's Chinatown, she focuses on the series of signifiers – her clothes, wedding ring, details of her education and job – that parallel and contextualize her status as mad. 'With these', she observes, 'I am trying to say that I am a wife, I am a good patient, I am an entrepreneur. I am also schizoaffective, living with schizoaffective disorder, living with mental illness, living with mental health challenges, crazy, insane – but *I am just like you*.'[31] The coincidental repetition – and Wang's own italicizing – of the central assertion in Grue's title is striking, but more important is that she is articulating a contradiction that is also surely perfectly recognizable. This is precisely an example of the kind of disability/ same discussed in the last chapter, and here it emerges as the kind of paralleling that is explored most fruitfully through Disability Studies approaches to complex subjectivities.

Fusions

When I think about these kinds of contradictions, my attention is always drawn back towards Lauren Slater, the most slippery of writers on schizophrenia and other conditions of mental illness, someone who both inhabits the worlds of the mad and views it from the clinical space that treats those worlds, naming it from each. As *Lying* makes clear, the only way this is possible for Slater is to embrace others forms of bending: fabrication, rule-breaking, deferral, and even (especially) dishonesty. These are techniques she carried forward to her writing about schizophrenia itself: as Slater worked more with the schizophrenic patients she encountered in *Welcome to my Country*, she revised her idea of the men being 'grotesques', mentioned earlier. After an evening spent reading academic articles on delusions, she notes that there were many on grandeur and paranoia, 'but nowhere does the literature mention delusions that weave around the themes of longing and loss, of great space and tundra'. She continues: 'Why? I wonder. Is it that the schizophrenic experience seems so bizarre to us, we can't imagine such a patient might be suffering from something as common as loneliness?' Schizophrenics may experience a 'heightened sense of isolation' but for Slater, a consequence is that this produces a 'keen desire to connect'. The condition's manifestations of fantasy are in fact about 'finding fusion', she asserts.[32] Loneliness and connections revise the idea of chaos; they ground the idea of the schizophrenic vortex. The 'common' is a word – and world – for everyone. It is another example of Jan Grue's 'living a life like yours'.

Slater's 'finding fusion' makes me think of Medical Humanities' commitment to entanglement and Disability Studies' advocacy of intersectionality. But neither of these is quite right in this context. I understand the entanglement/risk frame to be primarily about movements between subject areas, challenging and offering revisions. The intersections that tell more and better narratives about disability are about overlapping experiences and structural forms, from personal testimony to race or sexuality, or the spaces society creates for these, for example. But Slater's fusion is about the acts of connection in the very presence of or within schizophrenia, with all the complexities that come when something is *in front – or part – of you*. It is a fusion that might be at work when the chair encounters the stairs it cannot take, or an event causes stimming to increase, or the streets and houses start to bend. It is a kind of 'what happens next?' moment *of the common*; a theoretical position of the intersection and entangled but speaking in different ways.

Fusion is an enabling idea when considering Jonathan Caouette's 2003 film *Tarnation*, the documentary he made of his relationship with his schizophrenic mother Renee and his own experience of borderline personality traits. Formally, *Tarnation* is fusion in action. It is temporality and topography thrown into the air and sliced into new patterns as they fall. The film is edited from hundreds of hours of home movies, answering-machine tapes, excerpts from television, family photos, filmed friends, and footage of high-school productions, all from Caouette's past and interlaced with a kaleidoscope of challenging colourful images and dissonant music. It also gives a central space to Jonathan's own performances: whether re-enacting a panicked phone call to a hospital to check his mother's state following a Lithium overdose (the film starts with this, a moment of fiction and acting that unsettles the documentary modes that follow), in the many budget short horror films he made as a teenager, or in multiple pieces to camera. The most memorable of these last is when a (real) eleven-year-old Jonathan plays a young teenage wife – Hilary – who gives a testimony recounting how she killed her husband after a night of abuse. Poorly/strangely lit and with Jonathan in costume and makeup, fidgeting and acting distressed, it is an extraordinary viewing experience. It suggests the instability, dysregulation, intense disturbance and impulsiveness that make up the clinical definitions of BPD, but with these qualified by the recognition that Caouette is the controlled maker of everything we see: the writer, director, cinematographer and performer. It is controlled and produced schizoid art.

While this might seem as far away from Slater's 'common' as it's possible to get, it's not. *Tarnation*'s brilliance lies in its ability to take the whirlwind of which it's made and show that all of this makes sense because at heart it is a film about Jonathan's relationship with his mother and his desire to care for her. Renee's schizophrenia (clearly caused by a catastrophic series of electric shock therapy prescribed after injuries she received as a child when falling off the roof of the family home) is presented as the source of all the film's substance; it is in interacting with the condition that Jonathan finds his way to the common that can allow a son to connect to a parent. This is most obvious, but also most disturbing, in the longest scene in the film, in which for three and a half minutes Jonathan films Renee, in a single shot, holding a pumpkin and repetitively singing one modified song line from the Mexican folk song *La Cucaracha* in which the word *cucaracha* is replaced by 'pumpkin'. Renee's performance seems nonsensical, punctuated by howls of laughter and jerky physical dance movements the source of which cannot be understood; it is as bizarre (to return to Slater's word) as it is possible to imagine.[33]

What makes this worse is that the filming is intrusive: Jonathan's camera stays on his mother, apart from two pans to show objects – plates on the wall, a Christmas tree – that stress the setting is domestic and familial, and the whole is simply *too long*. Nearly all viewers I have spoken with feel the same as I do when watching. You just want it to stop. We've got the point: schizophrenia is very disturbing, it's frightening. Can we please just move on? And then you start to wonder about the ethics of the whole scene, about questions of consent and propriety, about Caouette's responsibility as a filmmaker and not just his presence as a son. But in fact, upon reflection, it's clear that this works in reverse: Caouette is *primarily* the creator and maker of the film – *Tarnation* is about as much the production of a single, auteurist, vision as a film can get – and in the pumpkin scene it is his presence as a son that nudges the disturbance towards the common, the family Christmas holiday complete with song and laughter. In a 2004 interview with *The Guardian*, Caouette spoke specifically to the tension of this scene: 'People are like, 'My God, you just didn't take the camera away.' It's so overwhelming and crazy to watch [...] The thing about that scene is that her and I were actually having a lot of fun. It communicates something else to other people.'[34] The family focus makes more sense when considering the overall arc of the film, which at its conclusion brings Renee to Jonathan's apartment in New York, where he and his boyfriend care for her, love her and try to make her happy and less lonely.

Understanding *Tarnation* demands questions of the critical frames that allow its depiction of schizophrenia to be read. The film is told through the kind of found fusion that Slater highlights, and it is Caouette's understanding of this and his translation of this fusion – his agile, indisciplined aesthetics – into the film's form that makes it so powerful. By coincidence, *Tarnation* appeared the year after *A Beautiful Mind* and when in *The Guardian* interview Caouette observes that 'there's so many movies now that candy-coat mental illness and it's such a crazy, complex thing', he could well be describing Howard's film. Here, crazy and complex are vital, productive terms. Crucially, they don't deny Renee's 'craziness' – her delusions, paranoia, psychosis, all of which we see – but rather make it possible to use these as creative tools for an encounter with schizophrenia.

The situating of storytelling in the world suggested by Renee's experiences is a representation of the productive ways in which Disability Studies configures the multiplicities of life narratives. Central to this is the combination of materiality and innovative form, a complimentary whatness and howness that reveals such stories. For over a decade and a half, Disability Studies scholarship has explicitly reconfigured the material body, from Tobin Siebers' ground-breaking formation of complex embodiment, through the incorporation of new materialist perspectives and disability-led intersectionalities, to the development of specific modes of crip affect. Such thinking is wonderfully productive, continually alive to the relationship between material objects – including bodies – and their representations. Theorizing crip versions of affect incorporates disability configurations of phenomenology and biopower in its focus on the body and that with which it comes into contact. Without a beat, it rejects the Cartesian dualism that would see the cognitive separated from the embodied, knowing that mental health is always material and marked as embodiment.[35] The pumpkin scene in *Tarnation* exemplifies this.

Critical Medical Humanities scholarship asserts that approaches to mental health based in psychiatry need to be reworked and that this is a process involving multiple pathways. There is a drive to unpick and rethink the language of diagnosis, to complicate what is meant by therapy (pyscho-, biblio-, talking-, drug-) and restorative models provided by Arts and Health models, and to problematize the idea of recovery narratives and their presumed status as the most beneficial outcomes of mental health treatment, just to name some topics.[36] Work undertaken in these areas is enlightening and challenging, but it is fundamentally *revisionist*. Its frame of critique is within the subjects and terms it addresses and doesn't have the creative critical imagination that drives Disability Studies thinking around mental health, the commitment to bending time, bodies and delusions that makes them complex, theorize and fused states.

To take an example of a comparison between the disciplines: 'psychosomatic' is a standard medical term for the interaction between mind and body. It is a curious coupling, as each half has evolved precisely through a distancing of the other: 'somatic' means body, especially because of its distinction from the mind, and vice versa. Though conjoined, there is no suggestion of a hybrid. Psychosomatic Disorder or Somatic Symptom Disorder is a condition, included in the *DSM*, where a patient will focus excessively on the thoughts around and feeling of being ill in ways that can be seen as out of proportion to the symptoms experienced. This is not a case in which a patient might be faking illness, but rather is experiencing it atypically. While diagnosis might involve psychiatric attention, treatment – the condition can cause anxiety, distress and often long-term depression – comes largely from primary care physicians; a twin (but not-hybrid) approach that covers its multiple manifestations. From the foundational collision of its two terms onwards, the complexities of psychosomatic are clear: it is rich ground for an investigation of bodies, minds, medical authority, and methods of treatment (just to name some topics) but there is no critical theory from within Medical Humanities that discusses the kinds of overlaps it exemplifies with anything like the investigative power of an idea such as Sami Schalk's 'bodyminds reimagined', a deliberate rule-changing mode of analysis that rethinks the psycho/cognitive and somatic/embodied through a disability lens.[37] It is the critical imagining of Schalk's work that succeeds here. In the same way that she can join body and mind to become a single word, Schalk's disability scholarship forms a productive union that is *unimaginable* in the conjoining of psycho and somatic.

Tarnation's subject matter is mental ill health, but it's a film obsessed with the material; with bodies, objects, and the ways that they're performed. Jonathan's body is continually on display, either through his direct pieces to camera or excerpts from films and photographic stills in which he features. He is bodyminds in action, an often-queer exposure of endlessly mobile physical selfhood matched by cascading behaviour that invites speculation as to his state of mind. Jonathan screams, grimaces, cries, laughs, vogues, fakes, embarrasses, questions, provokes, flirts and challenges – all within distorted image and soundscapes and for a camera that he ultimately controls. Tellingly, details of his own diagnosis, institutionalization and suicide attempts are given to viewers through the intertitles that break up the film, used mainly to provide temporal markers and medical details. These are given in clear prose, but if as watchers we want to understand *why* Jonathan was diagnosed with BPD, we have to make sense of the riot of his presence and try to read his psychological state through his actions, a challenge he knows he manipulates. Understanding this helps in a return to think again of Renee and her actions in the pumpkin scene. Renee's singing, laughing and jerky half-dances are no riot, and their filming is slow and (too) contemplative. The scene appears to scream mental illness and a seemingly broken mind, but in the context of *Tarnation* as a whole, these suggestions are made material by Renee's embodied presence and the impossible-to-ignore central fact of the pumpkin, the physical object that invites discussion and interpretation, but in the end appears most of all to be just *there* – the thing of the scene.

Living with

Tarnation is boundary-crossing and challenging. It *feels* radical and a visceral exposure, through its forms, to a schizophrenic mind. The fact that it was made in 2003 doesn't diminish the impact – depicting madness like this is still unusual, still outside of the mainstream[38] – but the date does prompt thoughts about how the digital and social media generation that has followed in the last twenty years figures schizophrenia, given the new proliferation of methods available for telling life stories. The user-led openness of blogs, vlogs and podcasts, and the possibilities of immersive technological experiences, seem to offer constructive possibilities for depicting and discussing the condition: take the lid off, say what's on (and in) your mind without it having to be filtered, don't be beholden to the rules and regulations of conventional storytelling, dive within a world. All of these feel that they might be open to the indiscipline of schizophrenia's chaos.

As ever, things are more complex. Search for the 'best schizophrenia vlogs' (and I deliberately went for this term as a critical move, rather than choosing those I know might align with my own sympathies) and those that come up are full of instructive contradictions. The YouTube channel *Living Well With Schizophrenia* is one of the most popular. It is a slick, well-made product that garners hundreds of thousands of views, with multiple high-production value videos featuring founder and creator Lauren Kennedy's personal experiences of her schizoaffective disorder. The power of Kennedy's articulate testimonies is tangible, containing not only specific details of, for example, her diagnoses, suicide attempts, delusions or hospitalizations, but also associated feelings of guilt, shame, embarrassment and stigma. Each video offers a down-to-earth narrative of what living with schizophrenia can be like, and comments below the line frequently display viewers' gratitude to Kennedy for her sharing and at finding sources of hope and inspiration.[39] At the same time, and even as it stresses that happy endings are not central to mental health recovery, *Living Well With Schizophrenia* follows some predictable trajectories: academic and employment success, personal relationships and parenthood, even the popularity of the videos themselves and the opportunities they have offered Kennedy to 'live well'. Aligned with this last is the clear monetization of the content. The site offers viewers the chance to become patrons where, for a fee, they will be able to access specific peer support and therapy groups. Another link is to merchandise – clothing, mugs, buttons. The videos don't 'sugar-coat' the complexities of living with the condition (a line from one of Kennedy's introductory pieces) but they do ask you to buy things. Somewhat insidiously, part of this is that payment grants access to additional videos and *more* recovery possibilities.

Kennedy's appeal is communicated through her appearance and the controlled fluency of her delivery. Filmed almost exclusively in head shots, she has the kind of telegenic presence associated with an information programme or news host. Kennedy is the perfect combination of distanced narrator and approachable confidante, so that schizophrenia (as she tells it) emerges as a life-threatening condition that causes despair but also a set of articulate stories to be shared. Beyond being photogenic, Kennedy's body plays no part in the videos of *Living Well With Schizophrenia*. She doesn't move, and her stillness is part of the calm authority her communication produces. Schizophrenia here is nothing to do with fragments, splitting, bending or the terrors of disassociation, the lights and sound cacophonies of *Tarnation*. It is rather conveyed through the clarity of a single speaking voice. Clarity is not something schizophrenia is supposed to have. Indeed, the condition appears to constitute the very opposite: hallucinations and delusions deceive, not clarify; psychosis is a state in which the clear is replaced by fog, and worse. It is important to know that this does not have to be the case however, and for all that *Living Well With Schizophrenia*'s videos tell stories of recovery and restitution (even if its stressed that these are provisional) part of success of the site is to show how people with schizophrenia are articulate and erudite, and how lived lives are possible.

Certainly I would sooner listen to Kennedy and other similar vlogs than read the seemingly never-ending negativity found in Solomon's *Far From the Tree*. In his book's chapter on schizophrenia, Solomon presents a succession of family vignettes that are a litany of despair and destruction. Each follows the same pattern: a brilliant, high-achieving teenager, popular, good at sports and destined for an Ivy League university (it is extraordinary how often this last is present) has their life shattered by the onset of the condition. Young men and women become deluded, violent, feral individuals, unknown to both their families and themselves. Time and again, Solomon stresses the tragedy of the life that appears to be lost, the 'descent into a deepening hell' that becomes the end point of the stories he narrates. People disappear, lost within the schizophrenic onslaught, and loved ones recount how love and relationships become impossible with zombified victims. 'How can you keep on loving a son who can be an unpleasant stranger?', Solomon records one father saying, while a mother observes: 'These kids die but they never get buried.' Both comments are typical of the impression of schizophrenia Solomon wants his readers to take away. Though he discusses underfunded treatment and recovery programmes, the Mad Pride movement, the complexities of medication, and questions of stigma and prejudice, it's impossible to come away from *Far From the Tree* with anything other than the feeling that, as one parent Solomon interviewed put it, schizophrenia is a form of death.[40]

This is predominantly a point about Solomon's approach, but it is also something that happens because of the medium in which that approach is manifest. *Far From the Tree* carries (literal) weight. It is over 950 pages, packed with detailed research and garlanded with the kind of prizes and praise that circulate within the economy of literary achievement. Endorsements come from Bill Clinton, previous Nobel Prize winners, and media outlets from across the globe. The book has all the authority that comes with such scaffolding, yet I find it a hateful account, one not only always searching for despair in the people to whom Solomon speaks, but crafting it through the writing and editing process, something that is *specifically* a technique of literary writing, editing and publishing. Part of Solomon's method is his incessant framing of all aspects of schizophrenia within medical typologies. Accounts of clinical approaches to the condition – data, developments in treatment, interviews with psychiatrists and academics – surround and enclose the family stories, making them seem even more desperate, deprived of space in a suffocating swirl of specialist knowledge. Here then is a 'medical model', but less one of *knowing* the body and mind through a unified field of reference, and more the *telling* of life stories, within literary structures, in which a recourse to expertise continually quantifies and codifies experience. In its monumentality and with the power of its seeming objectivity, *Far From the Tree* serves to remind that the first-person tellings of hope and recovery that are the stuff of blogs and vlogs, even those that promise happy(er) endings and possibly misrepresent mental illness, name more positive spaces than exist in the authoritative medical tradition in which Solomon works.

For some, *Far From the Tree* is exactly the kind of work that typifies Medical Humanities. In this view, the book marks an intervention into medical debates that stresses the human 'element', with Solomon a listener tuned into the human; a compassionate witness to the struggles of people with schizophrenia and their families and writer who humanizes the experiences of those encountering the condition, offsetting the technical terms of psychiatry with the real words of people. While such a view is not one that most close to the subject would hold (and I would think none who subscribe to its critical model), it is nevertheless an intellectual and practice-based position common in many who work in medicine and health. And of course it reaches an audience far in excess of the other writing examples I've mentioned in this chapter.

There are other ways to configure experiences of medicine that don't have the crushing inevitability Solomon narrates, however, and again these can be found within the open forms of user-made formats. In 2019, MindFreedom International, a US-based mental health rights organization, created a set of videos entitled 'Voices for Choices' that bring together thirteen short films exploring multiple topics: the history of psychiatric treatment and institutionalization, first-hand experiences of involuntary admission and medication use, and alternative models of healing and routes towards survivor activism.[41] Like *Living Well With Schizophrenia*, 'Voices for Choices' is based around the possibilities inherent in open-manufactured content, although unlike Kennedy's vlog, MFI stresses its non-profit status and independence from any outside funding or influence.

'Voices for Choices' is led by those with experience of mental ill health, often schizophrenia and other conditions associated with psychosis. The videos mix talking-head interviews with frequently graphic film of historical treatment methods and footage taken from within hospitals of specific committals. Being detained involuntarily, one speaker says, was 'like landing on a different planet', while others note how following initial arrival in psychiatric hospitals they were dragged to wards, placed in seclusion, and subject to forced injections (for some, the effects of the medication – especially a loss of energy and focus – were internalized as being part of their illness, so that the treatment added to the disorientation and fear that in many cases were read as being psychosis). Evaluation and diagnosis, the speakers make clear, is highly context-dependent, not only along lines of gender, culture and race but even, as one notes, depending on during which doctor's shift you might be seen. Across the videos, individuals stress that the circumstances of involuntary commitment exacerbated their emotional vulnerability, which in turn led to more outbursts. In one distressing piece of footage obtained by MFI, a woman frees herself from restraints after stating multiple times that she needs to change her tampon and is then restrained forcibly again by a team dressed in full riot gear (including body armour and helmets with visors). Recounting graphic moments like these, the speakers testify that it clearly didn't matter to hospital authorities what effect the detention had on them as individuals, but that the process was obviously structured as one that required them to be 'under control'. The experience was, one person observes, 'essentially dehumanizing' and something she likens to sexual assault and torture. 'I don't know any locked wards that have ever been houses of healing,' another woman comments, possibly the most eloquent phrase in a litany of reflections on the abusive practices the speakers received.

The videos stress that, when released from forced care, many often have serious relapses because they are no longer on the drug regime prescribed in hospital. Some spoke of being taken by the police for regular injections, refusal of which would mean immediate re-hospitalization. Given that a major form of psychosis is a fear of being controlled or harmed by those in positions of power, it is inevitable that actions such as these can trigger new episodes. Medication is a subject to which the 'Voices for Choices' videos return on numerous occasions. Speakers point out that often committal can depend upon an individual's response to being told that medication is essential; to agree with this is a sign of competency, but to disagree as an act of autonomy – quite possibly on the basis of lived experience – is to be labelled incompetent and therefore subject to immediate detention. Another speaker notes that her mother had died because of kidney failure due to repeated forced doses of lithium as treatment for her schizophrenia, and thought it likely she would die from the same cause, but that there was no option for her to refuse treatment based on these grounds. You can refuse chemotherapy, she says, knowing that this will cause death, but there is no way to prevent compulsory and imposed treatment when committed, even though this can lead to critical and fatal illness. Again, it is the association of schizophrenia with a perceived lack of rationality, a terrifying excess, that makes such a situation seem logical.

Though the 'Voices for Choices' videos follow what is a recognizable documentary format, the user-made element gives them the power of advocacy and claim. There is no need for a 'balanced' portrayal here, because for MFI balance is a non-existent idea and category in processes where power is so blatantly one-sided. In their response to this, the speakers stress throughout their treatment in terms of the abuse of their human and civil rights and the subsequent resulting trauma. What is instructive for the arguments I'm making in this chapter is that MFI frames this rights-based discourse through its historical development, from the 1970s onwards, as an organization linked explicitly to the disability rights and other social change movements. All of the voices in the MFI videos articulate what is fundamentally a disability discourse: systemic prejudice, organizational oppression, and the public discrimination that accompanies it; and, in opposition, 'equal opportunity of mental and emotional well being for all', as the organization's website puts it. Schizophrenia, as it emerges from the testimonies here, is a term created from within a structural incomprehension of the actual nature of mental health. In place of Solomon's role as an onlooker of despair in *Far From the Tree*, the survivors of 'Voices for Choices' present as activists in the fight against a medical system of incarceration that is more punitive than prison.

The video testimonies are part of oral history traditions central to the development of Disability Studies from the 1970s onwards. They not only speak of the actualities of institutionalized experience but, in the ways in which many of the survivors have gone on to become activists, enact the 'nothing about us without us' tradition of demanding social change. They stress community in a world where it is common to be defined through individual isolation. This may not be expressed in the *language* of some critical disability positions I have advocated in this chapter, the bent time of Kafer's writing or biopolitics as configured by Mitchell and Snyder (though it is connected to their crip potential), but in its emphasis on activism and inclusion it is further evidence of the explanatory power of seeing schizophrenia and psychosis within disability categories and traditions. As the MFI website states, the organization has been recognized as 'the epicenter of the mad movement', and 'mad' here is clearly a word more about disability pride than being medically ill, or a public slur.

Conclusion: Schizofutures

In an age of ever-expanding digital technology, what might future life narratives of schizophrenia look like and how might academic work on health and disability respond to them? A seemingly never-ending proliferation of technologies creates multiple opportunities for increased interactions with people, whether directly through such objects as wearables and gaming devices, the onslaught of social-media platforms, or wider insidious forms of state-sponsored data capture. It's dizzying to try to think of how these will reflect the growing public perception of mental illness. Maybe there will no longer be an audience for the kind of book Saks has written, and the vlogs I have discussed will be old school modes of expression, still just people talking out loud. For some, technology already has the capacity to convey the actual experience of conditions such as schizophrenia. The complexity of immersive technologies, especially the use of sensory modalities in the extended and wraparound worlds of augmented and virtual reality, conjure up the possibility of capturing what schizophrenia feels like. If it is defined by voices, hallucinations and delusion, then AR's combination of digital information and real-world environments, or the submergence central to VR, where sounds and images can come from anywhere and take any form, seem perfect spaces in which to understand a schizophrenic view of the world. Multiple engagement options will presumably be available: you might want to visit the experience because you have a real desire to know what schizophrenia is and to empathize and learn (for a school project, for example), or maybe you can drop in as part of a role-playing fantasy. Treatment and therapy could even be developed through the use of such technologies.

Goliath is a twenty-five-minute animated VR experience, made in 2021 by Barry Gene Murphy and May Abdalla for the Anagram creative studio, and can be watched through the Oculus Quest and HTC Vive headsets. It focuses on the schizophrenia of a single man (known only by his gamer moniker, Goliath) and his journey from a vulnerable child to acceptance and community in the online gaming world. The film recounts a chronological personal history, from childhood into addiction and then institutionalization, before gaming provides a pathway to stability. It features a low-key but powerful voiceover, in which Goliath describes each stage of his life up to the point of the film's making. He talks of his time as a carer for his disabled mother, as a techno DJ when a young man, the six years of involuntary committal that followed a breakdown, and the support from fellow gamers that now helps him structure his life.

It is of course the visuals that make *Goliath* distinctive. When Goliath talks about the arcade games he played as a teenager, the viewer has to use hand controllers to move a protagonist through a set of streets that is a replication of a 2D game world, encountering opponents from classic 1980s games such as *Streetfighter*. Later, when Goliath narrates how gaming allowed him connection to new friends, the viewer again becomes engaged, this time in classic shooter mode (hitting green symbols for friends and red for enemies). The time as a DJ is full of bright symbols and colours that fragment and fall away – accompanied by cascading letters – following a psychotic episode. In contrast, a series of voice descriptions of schizophrenia are accompanied by columns of falling words that surround the user, overlapping and overwhelming, forcing a series of head turns to try to catch the specific commentaries. Goliath's time in hospital is represented as a pink/orange body shape set in a naturalistic-style black/grey room more reminiscent of a prison than a care facility. This last section is especially powerful, with Goliath's orange body suddenly multiplying and falling through the dark spaces of the institution as his illness increases. At the film's end, the viewer is positioned inside Goliath's apartment as he plays and interacts with friends (all of whom are revealed to be disabled). The naturalism of this space – a slightly shabby sofa, door to a kitchen, a television, and books on shelves – indicates the independence he has found in taking control of his own life.

For all that *Goliath* is a surround-experience of colour, sound and words, it isn't particularly 'immersive'. Near the start, the viewer is asked to record their name and this is then played back as an echo during the description of a psychotic episode. While this is moderately effective, it also feels a little like a gimmick and is an intervention not repeated elsewhere in the film. In part, the lack of immersion is about technical elements; using a headset, it's impossible to change the height of the viewing position and for all that film is a 360-degree experience, this relies on a static location from with the viewer turns. I wanted to walk around Goliath's apartment at the end, or to bend down, to explore where he now lives, but this is impossible; I'm looking *at* his room, and am not in it, for all the objects there are on all sides of me. *Goliath's* power then, is also a reminder of the limits of VR technology.

But because of this, the film doesn't attempt to say that it's possible to replicate what schizophrenia *feels like*. *Goliath* tells of a singular experience, but rejects the premise that viewers can genuinely inhabit the space of Goliath's own past, which is in fact most powerfully conveyed through his words. It's clear that this is also an ethical and aesthetic choice, and that Murphy and Abdalla recognize the dangers of voyeurism in depicting a sensitive subject such as mental illness.[42] *Goliath* achieves a balance rare in visual representations of schizophrenia, inviting an engagement with its otherness, the assured feeling of being 'mad' (as Goliath says himself), but refuses to turn this into sentimentality or melodrama. It is undoubtedly structured as a journey, but through its stress on the unique nature of a single story pushes back against the presumption that all journeys through mental ill health are trajectories of recovery. Like *Tarnation*, *Goliath* achieves its power and insight because of its structuring of sound, image and continuity. It doesn't pretend to claim that it replicates fully the intrusive voices or hallucinations of schizophrenia, despite what might appear to be the use of a technology that suggests this could be possible.

Goliath screened at numerous high-profile festivals, including Tribeca, Sundance, South by Southwest and Venice. It is part of a new wave of garlanded VR films that speak of the promise of new technologies to tell stories. How these will be stories of illness is yet to be determined, but it's clear that the perceived greater sophistication of such technology may well seek a subject in the multiple expressions of mental illness, especially given the recognition of a current mental health crisis. Any outcome of this development can still only be a matter of conjecture, though every user of *Goliath* I have spoken to has commented on the potential value of the film as an education tool, especially for young adults and practising clinicians and healthcare workers.[43] Given the history of representing schizophrenia, however, there's every reason to believe that future stories of the condition will be more like those of *A Beautiful Mind*, with which I started this chapter: humanist, individual-centred narratives that focus on personal willpower and recovery, reducing experience to damaging cliché. The 360-degree version of that would truly be too much to bear.

I'm an optimist and feel that there's maybe a natural beat in this transition to a new paragraph in which I might suggest that the above point can be followed by something positive, that new technologies will provide more insightful and ethical depictions of schizophrenia and other forms of mental illness, especially in the hands of developers, such as Anagram, committed to such depictions. But it should be acknowledged that there is no real reason to believe this, beyond hoping that it might be so. Cinema is hardly an 'old' technology, especially in its digital forms, so to somehow consign it to the past and champion VR or AR makes no real sense. If, as Esmé Wang says, schizophrenia 'terrifies', then for all that education about the condition might improve, it will probably continue to do so and fear will mean that most people won't want to go anywhere near it. They are likely only to agree to engage with stories where any exposure to that terror is sorted and made good, where it's safe to watch or use and you can leave untainted.

Although it feels at times like a soft fallback position, I want to believe that hope, and particularly the work that hope inspires, remains valuable: hoping that medical science will help understand schizophrenia better; that healthcare systems will become adequate spaces of care; that a recognition of the ongoing effect a world-changing event is having on mental health will be sustained; and that a proliferation of stories across multiple ways of telling will mean that damaging stereotypes can be corrected. These kinds of changes have happened before with other health conditions and hoping and wanting it to happen with schizophrenia, imagining and working towards it happening, doesn't have to be passive. To articulate it is to name it as a possibility, to take part in a design for the future. It is still a critical undertaking, still theory in action.

Notes

1. It's worth noting that as part of its emphasis on individual achievement, *A Beautiful Mind* ignores that the prize was in fact shared with two others – John Harsanyi and Reinhard Selten – for work on the analysis and subsequent development of equilibria in the theory of non-cooperative games. While Nash's work was foundational to this, it was the ways in which Harsanyi and Selten extended his equilibria that established game theory as a major model of economic thinking.

2. 'Interview with Dr John Nash at the 1st Meeting of Laureates in Economic Sciences in Lindau, Germany, September 1–4, 2004'. Interviewer, Marika Griehsel. Nash's comments start at 25:08 and he continues: 'So it doesn't correspond to me accurately. It has been many years – I haven't had medicine since 1970'. Available online: https://www.nobelprize.org/prizes/economic-sciences/1994/nash/interview/ (accessed 17 September 2021).

3. Sander L. Gilman, *Difference and Pathology: Stereotypes of Sexuality, Race and Madness* (Ithaca, NY, and London: Cornell University Press, 1985), 23.

4. Nathan Filer, *The Heartland: Finding and Losing Schizophrenia* (London: Faber & Faber, 2019), 4–5.

5. Susanna Kaysen, *Girl, Interrupted* (London: Virago, 2000), 151.

6. Esmé Weijun Wan quotes Solomon in her collection of essays, *The Collected Schizophrenias* (London: Penguin, 2019), 28.

7. Lauren Slater, *Welcome to My Country: A Therapist's Memoir of Madness* (London: Penguin, 1996), 5.

8. W. Hall, G. Andrews and G. Goldstein, 'The Costs of Schizophrenia', *Australian and New Zealand Journal of Psychiatry* 19 (1985): 3.

9. W.J.T. Mitchell, *Mental Traveler: A Father, a Son, and a Journey Through Schizophrenia* (Chicago: University of Chicago Press, 2020), 112 and 14.

10. Wang, *The Collected Schizophrenias*, 3.

11. The virtual 2021 SIRS conference took place over five days and attracted nearly 1,000 researchers from fifty-one countries.

12. In October 2021, a piece in *Schizophrenia Research* asked: 'Are we ready for a name change for schizophrenia?', exploring the question from a variety of viewpoints with multiple stakeholders.

13. Jonathan M. Metzl, *The Protest Psychosis: How Schizophrenia Became a Black Disease* (Boston: Beacon Press, 2009), 94.

14. Vanessa Lawrence et al., 'Navigating the Mental Health System: Narratives of Identity and Recovery Among People with Psychosis Across Ethnic Groups', *Social Science and Medicine* 279 (2021): 1, 8. Available online: https://doi.org/10.1016/j.socscimed.2021.113981 (accessed 10 January 2022).

15. Wang, *The Collected Schizophrenias*, 39.

16. Ibid.

17. Ibid., 29–30.

18. The metaphor of travelling is so prevalent in mental health memoirs that it's impossible to list how many use it. As I write this, two are immediately within reach on my desk: Kate Millet's *The Loony-Bin Trip* (New York: Simon & Schuster, 1990) and Patrick and Henry Cockburn's co-produced *Henry's Demons: A Father and Son's Journey Out Of Madness* (London: Simon & Schuster, 2011).

19. Wang, *The Collected Schizophrenias*, 11.

20. Elyn R. Saks, *The Center Cannot Hold: My Journey Through Madness* (New York: Hachette Go, 2020), 13.

21. Saks, *The Center Cannot Hold*, 110.

22. Ibid., 35.

23. Arnhild Lauveng, *A Road Back From Schizophrenia* (New York: Skyhorse, 2020), 3.

24. Lauveng, *A Road Back From Schizophrenia*, 166–7 and xi.

25. Saks, *The Center Cannot Hold*, 336.

26. Ibid., 349–50.

27. Rudy Tian, 'Three Puzzles Explainable With My Experience', *Schizophrenia Bulletin* 48, no. 1 (2022): 6–7.

28. Peter Beresford, '"Mad", Mad Studies and Advancing Inclusive Resistance', *Disability and Society* 35, no. 8 (2020): 1340.

29. Beresford, '"Mad", Mad Studies and Advancing Inclusive Resistance', 1339.

30. Alison Kafer, *Feminist, Queer, Crip* (Bloomington and Indianapolis: Indiana University Press, 2013), 27. Although Susanna Kaysen is discussing Borderline Personality Disorder and not schizophrenia, I like her distinction between 'velocity' and 'viscosity' in *Girl, Interrupted* as a way of talking about the different speeds of mental ill health.

31. Wang, *The Collected Schizophrenias*, 45. Italics in original.

32. Slater, *Welcome to My Country*, 19–20.

33. The scene can be found here: https://www.youtube.com/watch?v=YEY1JeP6FvU (accessed 6 December 2021).

34. Skye Sherwin, 'Up Close and Personal'. *The Guardian*, 21 May 2004. Available online: https://www.theguardian.com/film/2004/may/21/cannes2004. cannesfilmfestival (accessed 7 January 2022). For all that Caouette's point about shared happiness in the scene might be true, Sherwin calls it 'excruciating', which I think is a more common response.

35. For an excellent collection of essays on this topic, see *The Matter of Disability: Materiality, Biopolitics, Crip Affect,* ed. David T. Mitchell, Susan Antebi, and Sharon L. Snyder (Ann Arbor: University of Michigan Press, 2019).

36. For a discussion of this last within an explicit Critical Medical Humanities frame, see Angela Woods, Akiko Hart and Helen Spandler, 'The Recovery Narrative: Politics and Possibilities of a Genre', *Culture, Medicine, and Psychiatry* 46 (2019): 221–47. Available online: https://doi.org/10.1007/s11013-019-09623-y (accessed 1 November 2021).

37. Sami Schalk, *Bodyminds Reimagined: (Dis)ability, Race, and Gender in Black Women's Speculative Fiction* (Durham, NC, and London: Duke University Press, 2018).

38. One of the elements that contributes to *Tarnation*'s status is undoubtedly its mythic reputation as one of the cheapest feature films ever made, put together entirely on iMovie and purportedly costing just over US$218. Whatever the truth of this initial figure, significant funding was made available after its acquisition by new producers for its distribution on the festival circuit.

39. Most of the videos, usually between eight and twenty minutes in duration, function in this way but thinking about the contents of this particular chapter, it was enjoyable to watch Kennedy's fifty-one-minute 'Is *A Beautiful Mind* an accurate portrayal of schizophrenia?'. Available online: https://www.youtube.com/watch?v=NonwXc7_kEM (accessed 17 September 2021).

40. Andrew Solomon, *Far From The Tree: Parents, Children and the Search for Identity* (London: Vintage, 2014), 329, 337.

41. See https://mindfreedom.org/knowledgebase/voices-for-choices-video-series (accessed 14 May 2022).

42. There is a caveat here. The film as a whole features a voiceover by the actor Tilda Swinton that – especially at the beginning and conclusion – creates a dramatic idea of reality and illusion that feels at odds with the rest of the production. 'The mind is a mysterious place,' Swinton says at the start, going on to state that 'Reality is a very serious business'. 'Reality is just a story. One we tell ourselves to make sense of the world,' she adds later, broadening this into a flat, banal statement that comes after Goliath finishes his story: 'All realities are imagined, but the ones we share endure.' Suggesting to the viewer that the reality outside of the experience is an illusion is fundamentally a gimmick and nowhere near as interesting as Goliath's intricate narration of his own madness: 'the universe is revolving around me, in a bad way,' he says at one point, in a far more illuminating phrase. It's impossible not to feel that Swinton's involvement is primarily an addition that helped make the film more marketable.

43. *Goliath* was shown as part of the 'Disability Futures' programme at the 2022 Leeds International Film Festival. From 15–16 November, over fifty people saw the film. Those I spoke to as they came out of the experience all spoke of the power of Goliath's journey and the role the film could play in educating a wider audience about schizophrenia.

REFLECTION 3: STRAPS

The fields around the border between Germany and the southern Netherlands are undemonstrative. Featureless and flat, they are either producing crops or lying in wait to do so. Today it is the latter, and the land is fallow. It's the mid 1970s: I am eight or nine and in a car with my father, driving to visit my mother. On the straight roads he allows me to sit in the front and change gear, a ridiculously exciting act for a boy who watches being a grown-up from a distance. Though we have made this trip before, we have had no explanation or discussion about why, beyond 'going to see Mum', but the experience I get of nearly driving renders this irrelevant. In those moments, getting my timing right as he presses down the clutch is all that matters.

My mother is in the psychiatric ward of Wegberg military hospital, which caters for British Forces personnel and is a few miles outside the Royal Air Force base in Germany near which we live. The ward is in a separate unit to the main hospital, so on arrival we skirt the squat buildings that house the regular facilities and head for an even more nondescript concrete structure. Surrounded by neatly tended bushes, it is stained grey by the damp that has seeped up from the ground.

After the necessary clearances, we enter the all-female ward. I am a figure of great interest. Many of the middle-aged women there recognize me from previous visits and come up and surround me. There are comments about how nice it is to see me again and more than one kiss on the cheek. This is mortifying but inevitable, something that's become a bit of a ritual. It is nice to break away and head for my mother's bed. Today however she is not there and my father is told that she is in a separate room, having not been well in the night.

For all that they invest in disguise, no psychiatric hospital – and certainly not a military hospital in the 1970s – can shift the feelings that hang in the air. A mix of unconvincing comfort and threatened correction prevails, and tension, foreboding and a deep unsettlement are everywhere. This is especially true for a child and I pull into myself as we turn down hallways lined with white tiled walls, doors opening on each side. The mix of silence and echo is unnerving. My mother sits up in her bed in a room at the end, pale but, as ever, with perfect *hair, and we greet each other with that strange awkwardness specific to hospital visits. There are the usual questions about how I'm getting on, but – embarrassed and looking away – my attention is drawn to the details of the sparse space: the bed, the cabinet to the left, and a single comfortable (plastic) armchair in the corner. The bed itself is strange, bulkier than her one in the ward and with straps hanging down that my sister later tells me are restraints. My sister also tells me that she remembers my mother having to be restrained on one occasion when she was convinced that people were putting out cigarettes on her skin, but on this visit I didn't know that, didn't know that she had psychotic episodes and was in all probability involuntarily detained here.*

For the most ordinary of reasons, my mother is an alcoholic. Speaking only English but living in a German village, not working but with a husband and children who leave the house every morning, she has no community, despite there being other British families on our street. Agoraphobic, she does not feel comfortable taking the twice-daily bus to the base and the village itself is not an option. My mother is a woman of her time, with strong memories of the war, and for her Germans are never to be trusted, always still the enemy. Morning sherry get-togethers are a lifeline but, precisely because they are one of the very few possibilities for conversation and exchange, they create enormous pressures for a woman whose mental health has been fragile since she was a teenager. Whether alone at home or vying for attention at a neighbour's house, the estrangement is pervasive. That both locations are places to drink is an obvious invitation to eradicate the feelings they create.

My father tells me that he would like to speak to my mother privately, so I get to leave the room and walk through the hallways. Most of the other rooms are empty, but one has a young man inside, sat on a bed and dressed in uniform. Perfectly naturally, he invites me in and we talk, but more than anything we say I am taken by a detail of his cap which lies on a table next to the bed. It is standard military issue, camouflage and peaked with a forehead space for a name. Written there in large capital black letters is the word Death. He tells me that he is a Corporal and I ask him if his name is Death, if he is Corporal Death. He laughs and says yes. With the benefit of hindsight, I have wondered if his name might have been D'eath, an unusual but not unknown surname. But I feel that this makes no sense. It may well be my ignorance and prejudice, but I cannot make the imaginative leap between this working-class soldier and a name I now almost wholly associate with the aristocracy. And besides, we are in a psychiatric hospital.

My father comes to find me and takes me back to my mother's room. We say goodbye and then navigate the main ward on the way out – I am made to promise to return with updates on all I have been doing, and there are more kisses – and then it is back to the car and the journey home.

I cannot say for certain that it occurred to me at any point during this visit and others like it that my mother was specifically mentally ill. We were clearly 'going to see' her but, lacking a reason, I had an empty space – one of her being sick (she was after all in a hospital) – rather than a cause. I knew that there had been scenes at home, arguments and visits from the Military Police because of 'domestic disturbances', but I had no idea of their origin or, in truth, of their meaning, beyond the upset caused. Likewise, my memory of Corporal Death is of the puzzle of his unusual name, rather than that this was in any way a manifestation of mental ill-health: he was lucid, engaged, articulate and funny. The women on the ward embarrassed me, but I was unable to get beyond that embarrassment to wonder as to why they were there. No one in the unit actually seemed unwell.

One result of my mother's multiple stays in Wegburg was a subsequent addiction to tranquilizers. She became another inhabitant of the world created by the explosion of benzodiazepines prescriptions – Librium, Mogadon, Valium – in the 1960s and 1970s, a world largely populated by women whose social and emotional wellbeing was misunderstood or ignored and who were clearly in need of support services and not medication. Rather than explore why such women found themselves in such crisis situations, a generation of clinicians saw benzodiazepines as wonder drugs that alleviated anxiety and 'calmed down' those who took them. Put all this in a conservative military environment, and it was a clear recipe for disaster. For my mother, the truth of such 'alleviation' became desperate cravings, paranoia, helplessness, a sense that she was unable to function without her medication, terror that the drugs might not be available, and a further dependency on alcohol. I cannot be sure, but I believe that there was every possibility that her brain was permanently affected by this combination of addictions. Certainly, her life was.

I'm aware that my observations are the perspectives of a child, or more accurately the memories of a child's perspectives, and that they are maybe as much about my father's silences as my mother's condition, but I still wonder how they speak of the possibility to know or not know, to try to see and come close to, mental ill-health. This is not a point about its supposed unintelligibility or mystery – nothing I have seen of mental illness have ever made me think of it in these terms – but more what takes place when it is not articulated, when words are not available, not specified (through shame or fear, or a simple lack of knowledge) and it cannot be named. Faced with the ongoing reality of my mother's long-term mental condition, I had no frame of reference for it and no way to recognize it. While it might seem that a visit such as that I describe could only be an encounter with mental health – all those signals, from the straps on a bed to the name on a cap – I sense it is a mistake to suggest that this is somehow obvious. And this is not only something a child might feel. In An Unquiet Mind, *her memoir of her madness, Kay Redfield Jamison recounts how during her training as a clinical psychologist she 'did not make any connection in my own mind between the problems I had experienced and what was described as manic-depressive illness in the textbooks [. . .] I blithely went on with my clinical training and never put my mood swings in any medical context whatsoever'.*[1] *If a clinician couldn't see it when it was right in front of her, what chance a boy who wasn't yet ten?*

Years later and living back in the UK, during a routine teenager–parent argument, I was provoked and angered enough to ask why I had never been told about my mother being ill in Germany, something I had never said before. It immediately went quiet. 'We didn't think you knew,' my father said, and it was clear – stunningly – that he meant it. The following day, my mother came to see me. In a rare moment of openness, she told me that she had hoped my question might have prompted some discussion with my father about that time and as she spoke, I realized that this was a conversation they had never had. Yes: of Wegberg, I thought, the restraints, the drinking and the Mogadon, the fear. 'He didn't say anything,' she added. It really is easy not to see and not to know; it may well be the easiest thing.

Note

1. Kay Redfield Jamison, *An Unquiet Mind: A Memoir of Moods and Madness* (London: Picador, 1995), 59–60.

CHAPTER 3
DISABILITY/BODIES/HEALTH/ MEDICINE

Not working

There's a common experience insufficiently discussed in the critical contexts of health and disability in which I work. It's one where what's most powerful are the consequences of medicine and healthcare's inability to work, where the fallout from behaviour becomes a messy and at times unnameable state of existence. Interventions and therapy can help, but may well be thought to be inadequate or even counterproductive. This is a complex patterning, one where desired personhood and unsuccessful remedy circle one another in unsettled shapes. That patterning is also an invitation for the critical processes of Disability Studies and Medical Humanities, one where theory and critique can offer lines of enquiry that help make sense of health questions and their meanings in the world. These experiences open up what I feel can be a difficult but necessary conversation, in which disabling conditions and chronic ill health can create pain and loss, often at a life-changing level. As part of this, I want to ask what is involved when medicine fails in identifying a problem, not simply because of the clinical complexities of the body, but also because its gaze misses some other vital element, something social or cultural – like gender, for example. Failed medical practice frequently adds to the difficulties that come from ill health and creates anger when that failure is realized and confronted, when it is then too late for treatment to be effective, or years have been lost to illness. There's a challenge to scholarship here: what do Medical Humanities and Disability Studies have to offer when all of these issues are in play, especially when – more than anything – what a person wants is to get better?

There are many conditions and events where health is compromised catastrophically and disability is unwanted. As examples, locked-in syndrome and Motor Neurone Disease (MND) each presents as a total experiences of bodily transformation, a process that almost always lead to death. Locked-in syndrome is usually caused by injuries to the brain through tissue loss as a result of bleeding or from a stroke. It is characterized by full-body paralysis, though the individual is conscious and aware, and cognitive function is unaffected. The only movement possible is that of the eyes (sometimes only one), though here there can be difference: either vertical movement only or both vertical and horizontal. Although research into the possible quality of life varies, arguably no condition is seen as more disabling in the public imagination, with the sudden onset of a total shutdown of the body's function understood as a flatlining of life. The immediate loss of mobility creates not only the sudden loss of the body, but a total shift to dependency that removes agency. The experience is often imagined from without as horrific, the instantaneous loss of the body combined with the profound psychological challenges that follow. In many ways, the absence experienced by those who have the condition is filled in by the power of the non-disabled imagining *of the unimaginable*, a tautology that nevertheless has considerable power. Pain, grief, pity, despair and anger are all emotions involved in facing the experience of life lived in this way. Few who live with locked-in syndrome get to tell their stories, yet one of the most famous of all disability memoirs, Jean-Dominique Bauby's *The Diving-Bell and the Butterfly*, does just that. Bauby's rich description of his dreams and what he at one point terms his cultivation of the 'art of simmering memories' is an extraordinary account of what he stresses is his 'continuing life', the power of continuity in a profoundly disabling experience.[1]

MND is also neurological, but progressive in its systemic expression. It is unstoppable, an incurable condition that affects the brain, nerves and muscle and worsens over time, leading inevitably to death, though the time period for the process and the ways in which the body is affected can vary considerably. MND (like Alzheimer's and other forms of dementia) is considered to be especially tragic because of its timeline, the slow erosion of capacity and functionality, the day-by-day reduction and loss of the person affected. The person with MND deals with both the daily difficulties and psychological turmoil caused by the inevitability of the one-way journey. In the memoir of his own experience with MND, Albert Robillard describes the frustration, isolation and anger he has had to deal with, as well as his fears for his family and the assumption of others that his real life existed only 'before' the onset of his condition. As with locked-in syndrome, MND necessitates complex patterns of care, usually involving family and health practitioners, which are best understood as structures of attention and labour. While it seems inevitable that the focus is always on the individual experience of a condition like MND, these intricacies of care should not go unacknowledged.

Two thoughts: first, it might seem that I have been guilty here of an act that I accused other Disability Studies scholars of earlier, namely cherry-picking examples of a disability experience to make a critical point, given that I'm choosing two rare conditions untypical of the majority of disability lives to discuss agency and selfhood in a specific way. But I would counter that while locked-in syndrome is indeed very uncommon, MND isn't. I was struck by a figure on the UK's Motor Neurone Disease Association website that gave additional scale to the usual '1 in a ...' description of a disease's frequency. 'If you have 10,000 people in a stadium', the website notes, '33 of them will get MND at some point across a normal lifespan'.[2] I felt this had great power, to imagine that in any large sporting event, concert, political rally, or similar gathering – the kind of thing that happens every weekend – 200 people will develop MND. Second, both Bauby and Robillard write, in different ways, extraordinary books, but they are very much exceptions. Most people with locked-in syndrome will die because of complications caused by the condition (as Bauby did) while the majority of those with MND die within five years. In fact, MND is only seen as uncommon precisely *because* most people who have it die from it relatively quickly. The frequency of its onset doesn't translate into a sizeable community of those living with the condition.[3]

Stop and go away

I also want to counter any suggestion of choosing untypical examples by doing exactly the opposite. The rest of this chapter will look at questions of chronic pain and the disabilities that accompany incurable conditions associated with women's bodies, many of which are common but characterized as 'unexplained'. I cannot focus on them all but nevertheless want to mention several here, to make a point about the poverty of knowledge and understanding that surround them. They include lupus, thyroiditis, coeliac disease, rheumatoid arthritis, myositis, cystitis and vulvodynia, as well as more specific conditions that surround menstruation and pregnancy, such as endometriosis, preeclampsia and HELLP syndrome, pelvic inflammatory disease, polycystic ovarian syndrome, hyperemesis gravidarum, and uterine fibroids.[4] Given that menstruation is a foundational and fundamental part of the bodily cycle, these are as common as it's possible to get, especially when it's remembered that menstruation affects, or will affect, the majority of the world's population.

All of the above are conditions that affect women (though men account for around 10–15 per cent of lupus cases) and nearly all manifest through pain. As the individual stories recounted by women tell time after time, these are health experiences routinely misunderstood and misdiagnosed, or sometimes not recognized at all. The world of which they speak is typified by a crashing failure to understand the body, often even to attempt to understand the body, truths that directly confront an inherent sexism in the practice of medicine. This failure has multiple repercussions: a systemic ignorance surrounding women's pain and refutation of their knowledge of their own bodies; a subsequent lack of research into the manifestations and experience of such conditions; and the negation of them as being as disabling. As many women have found, if there are doubts that something exists, how can you be disabled with it?

I'm aware that in writing this there is a danger of my perpetuating a discourse in which men write about women's bodies, but want to stress that the bulk of the chapter is given over to women expressing themselves about their own health. In addition, there is a danger here that critical thinking ends up focused only on the authenticity of experience, something that I feel is an over-simplification of health and disability and something scholars should push back against. I think that more men should know about periods and take time to find out about them. For me, the issue is not in who writes what, but whether the writing prioritizes a considered ethical approach and commits to an appropriate respect. I don't think that this is impossible and I certainly believe it should be attempted and encouraged.

My critical context for this discussion is a return to the ways in which Disability Studies and Medical Humanities approach the health and meaning of bodies. I sense that there is a significant absence of clarity that surrounds the conditions I mention above, one that revolves around experience, treatment, public perceptions, choice, and associated questions of selfhood so important to how people live with health, as well as the ways in which these are discussed in academic discourse. As with this book's previous chapters, I want to argue that thinking critically about a health topic – here endometriosis and menstruation in particular – can become an example of the limits of disciplinary thinking, a process in which assumptions are made about what a body does and what that means. I think that often there is a serious looking-away from, for example, the experience of a condition such as endometriosis when Disability Studies formulates ideas of disability identity, while it is blatantly clear that much practice of medicine fails drastically when tasked with encountering menstruation: not only looking-away but also a profound inability to see.

Much of this revolves around pain. I don't have the space to speak of and to the vast amount of critical literature that discusses pain – from the idea that its inexpressible to the notion that it's a surfeit of expression, from the ways it's measured to the suggestion that it can't be measured, from the manner in which it's located in the body to the recognition that it extends beyond the body, and so many more perspectives. What I want to focus on is the fact that *pain hurts*, what that means for those who experience such hurt, the ways in which those experiences are expressed, and how the academic perspectives that are the subject of this book address these factors. In particular, I want to argue that the relationship between pain and selfhood is an experience where the difference-of-disability argument falters. Continuous pain, such as that associated with lupus and endometriosis, disables in multiple ways. Changing all the time and often unpredictably, it can require radical modifications of thinking about what a body can do. Pain's elusiveness and volatility, its lack of any seeming logic, sometimes seems to be its only constant. And as the person in pain engages with medical and social worlds, they often encounter responses that are classically disabling: systems that cannot accommodate them, whether medication regimes or employment practices, and the bemusement or hostility that comes because they don't 'seem' disabled, especially when these reactions are associated with gender. People in pain fight all the time to make others understand how their world is different. It is a thankless, draining and often impossible task that can, in addition to its effect on the body, result in many associated mental health issues.

Thinking about social responses to pain as disability can miss the very basic point about hurt. Because pain can hurt to the extent that so much is impossible, from movement to thought to relations with others to any kind of place within a range of social environments, it creates waves of seemingly never-ending negatives that can totalize as the interruption and restriction of life. And because pain hurts so much, what the person in pain may understandably want is for it to go away, or at least to be reduced. In such a situation, they may well have no desire to associate with an identity that constitutes pain as disabled difference. Where then is the space for individual choice here? How is such choice respected, or not, in academic discourses that are highly suspicious of cure or being fixed? What's thought to be legitimate expression?

In asking these questions, I'm not for a second suggesting that they are not about structures. One of my reasons for focusing on conditions that cluster around menstruation is *because* they are so illustrative of the failure of health and care structures. An aspect of my argument is that in responding to this, we need to recognize that Medical Humanities and Disability Studies are themselves structures – of enquiry, evaluation, judgement – that form ideas of (here) women's experiences of their bodies. Just because there is, rightly, ferocious academic criticism of how medicine treats women doesn't necessarily mean that the counter arguments should escape scrutiny. The coming together of individual narratives of endometriosis or lupus with the systems of health practice and academic investigation is exactly one of the examples of naming a world that I have tried to stress in this book. One specification that emerges from this is that the structures of Disability Studies, especially its ideas of what constitutes disability experience, fail to capture how menstrual pain is a disability and, consequently, what a disabled body might be. Despite some of my arguments in the previous chapter about the ways in which Disability Studies theorizes the body and disability's materiality, a condition like endometriosis comes to be a limit cases of where those arguments can reach.

A central point here is the complexity with which pervasive disability can be theorized. Disability Studies' affirmative model of value promotes vigorous counter narratives to medical negatives and instead stresses presence, agency and voice; scholarship is fiercely articulate in asserting that to be disabled is to signal difference and not deficit. Absence, lack and loss – as they are applied to disability lives – are ideas shot through with ableism. They build in a pejorative understanding of the very foundational aspects of personhood and agency, and render disability as both less and unknown, positioned outside of the structures of power and opportunity. Activists, writers and scholars push back through detailing disability's complex processes of variability and productivity – crip time, reconfigured space, critiques of orthodoxy – that celebrate the crooked, mad and those subject to unjust discrimination. They honour lives, tell stories, challenge paradigms, petition governments and change laws so that disability is not seen as a tragedy.

Nevertheless, I want to contend that at times these systems of thought can paradoxically create forms of enclosure and restriction that don't allow for the complexities of experience to be expressed. Again, individual pain is central here. Much of the anger that women with autoimmune conditions such as endometriosis feel about frequent misdiagnosis is directed towards a medical system that is not fit for purpose in treating the condition, and here there is no doubt that the work undertaken by Disability Studies provides insight and language that needs to be heard so that practice is changed. But with endometriosis it is embodiment that dominates: physical pain so intense it spreads from a central gut ache throughout the body, down arms and legs, causing sweating so powerful that severe vomiting is common; the grinding pain of a heavy period that starts in the pelvis and affects everything you might want to do; a burning and stinging that comes with every visit to the toilet; the frequent experience of clothes soaked in blood. While it is a provocation to ask what Disability Studies might have to say about this, there is a much more important question: who wouldn't want such pain to go away?

This can be extended. What about those individual moments of health where someone feels strongly that something that was there has gone? It is a common disability experience for a function or sense that was central to vanish or become impaired and for the person who experiences this to desire more than anything to have it back. In such cases, loss may be impossible to ignore; in fact, it may sit squarely in the middle of all the feelings produced by the event. Lack here might be a formative, even foundational, element of a new subjectivity – the *thing* that can't be avoided. Bella Bathurst's wonderful memoir *Sound* is not about how she became deaf, but rather how she was *deafened*. Following an initial misdiagnosis that determined an accident caused her progressive deafness, Bathurst discovered twelve years later that in fact her hearing loss was the product of otosclerosis, a condition in which bones in the inner ear fuse together to impede the transmission of soundwaves. Otosclerosis is reversible through surgery and *Sound* concludes with Bathurst's return to a world of sound following an operation. Throughout the book, she is honest and open about 'being' deaf, documenting its challenges (one chapter is called 'Loss') and how it changed her perception of her world. At the end, she writes: 'All I had known during the time that I was deaf was that there was something missing, something I couldn't put my finger on'; it was 'something invisible', more than 'straightforward mechanical facts'.[5] But the fact that Bathurst equates her deafness with loss in this way doesn't mean she frames disability as an absence in any kind of totalising manner about her selfhood. *Sound* articulates a profound connection to the worlds of the deaf and Deaf, to spaces that deafen (across chapters she explores histories of music, construction, warfare and others), and to the mechanics of hearing. That Bathurst wanted her hearing back doesn't make her memoir ableist.

An assertion that Bathurst's twelve years of deafness should be seen as a productive difference may well be a powerful and positive reaction, a readjustment of expectation and experience. But it might also be patronising and ignorant, a failure to engage and imposition of values on someone who wants nothing more than to get back what has become absent, to return to a previous state. Even though examples like this may be understood as 'classic' disability – the loss of a limb, or function more widely, of a sense or capacity – it might be that, as with Bathurst's operation, medicine is a better and more productive frame than disability to speak to such circumstances. It is important here not to be seduced by the language of restoration and recovery, and vital to note that the very idea of 'getting better' can carry heavy neoliberal overtones of emphasising personal responsibility and downplaying the structural failures of healthcare. But isn't it possible to do this *and* recognize that if people don't feel as they want, they have a need and right to turn to medicine in order to get better? As Bathurst shows, getting better can be a pathway back to complexity, and not simply a recovery of a problematic form of wholeness.

Part of the provocation here is to supplement this argument about the limitation of Disability Studies with the assertion that it is the critical capacity of Medical Humanities that is well placed to attend to the experience of menstruation and its consequences. This might sound counterintuitive given my point about the spectacular failure of medical care to adequately diagnose and treat women in pain, but here the case to be made is that it is the ways in which Medical Humanities, as a critical discipline, seeks to *improve* an understanding of medicine that can create the possibilities of constructive theorising and scholarly address. It is often a criticism of Medical Humanities that it is too focused on medicine and medical practices and that it lacks sufficient understanding of social and cultural determinants of health, but when the discipline is at its most sophisticated that focus is an advantage. At its most complex, Medical Humanities is a dynamic and flexible set of academic approaches to manifestations of medicine and health. It includes models that investigate the processes of healthcare that are more nuanced than those academic studies of disability that cluster round uninterrogated assumptions of a medical model, and its emphasis on positive associations and entanglements position those processes within questions derived from fields that explore history, philosophy, biopolitics, developments in technology, narrative, imagination, or ideas of citizenship – to name just some. This is a formidable intellectual arsenal. Its concentration on how health *works* forms part of what Felicity Callard has termed 'the animating logics that braid the threads of the medical and the humanities together', a weaving of insight.[6]

To repeat something I stressed at the end of the Introduction, there's an obvious conceit that I'm indulging here to make a point: if the previous chapter found the critical language of disability models best suited to the expression of schizophrenia, that most medical of mental health conditions, here the disciplinary positions are flipped. Faced with articulated identities of disabling pain and the desire for that pain to be alleviated, I'm contending that it is Disability Studies' conceptions of what constitute a disabled body that are shown to be limited. I appreciate that this method might appear to re-inscribe a binary that keeps the disciplines apart, when I argued before that they were complex overlapping systems, but it's still possible to assert the latter while showcasing the former in order to *provoke*. I have chosen this structure because it speaks to my desire to use the workings of each to critique the success of the other and to (again) highlight how, despite the overlapping, there is much the disciplines do differently. Stories of women's bodies can show how.

Writing inside out

Women's bodies have always been misrepresented, disciplined and subject to correction. Elinor Cleghorn's cultural history *Unwell Women* is a blistering account of such error and prejudice from the Ancient Greeks to the present. Cleghorn finds that the mystification and misdiagnosis that accompany the treatment of women's bodies and illness are central to how medicine has been constructed and is still practised: 'gender myths', she notes, 'are ingrained as biases that negatively impact the care, treatment and diagnosis of all people who identify as women'. Such myths and the expectations that they create mean that healthcare providers and systems routinely fail women, especially when confronted with women's pain. Cleghorn continues: 'Women are more likely to be offered minor tranquillizers and antidepressants than analgesic pain medication. Women are less likely to be referred for further diagnostic investigations than men. And women's pain is much more likely to be seen as having an emotional and psychological cause, rather than a bodily or biological one.'[7]

Cleghorn's study is more than just a history. It is also an account of her own lupus, which went undiagnosed for seven years during which she experienced chronic pain in her legs and, later, across her back and shoulders, along with associated swelling, headaches and racing pulse. Initially dismissed as possible gout, a flare of hormones, or an unknown pregnancy,

Cleghorn's condition affected her actual pregnancies, specifically the development of her second son's heart. Suddenly subjected to a battery of tests when this was discovered, but still feeling that any problem was unconnected to her own pain because of the way in which it has been continually dismissed, and therefore not mentioning it, she was given tentative diagnoses of Sjögren's syndrome and peripartum cardiomyopathy before lupus was confirmed. Lupus explained everything, from Cleghorn's early pain to the realization that her second pregnancy had produced a flare of the condition, one that affected her unborn son when her autoantibodies were transferred to him and caused a congenital heart block. The diagnosis 'was devastating, but it was also a relief [...] Countless times I tried to explain my persistent pain and swollen joints to doctors only to have my symptoms written off [...] I'd been on the receiving end of withering glances, eye-rolls, smirks and heavy sighs [...] I started to believe that I must have been making it up, that the pain was all in my mind. Guilt and shame gnawed at me until I didn't trust my body any more.'[8] Given that lupus is thought to be a condition activated by a grouping of genetic and environmental factors, it seems a cruel mirroring that it is precisely the combination of inside and outside elements, manifested in Cleghorn's bodily pain and then the resulting social misunderstanding, which created this lack of trust.

Cleghorn's personal journey is a Medical Humanities intervention because she is a feminist historian who places her experience within the wider collective structures of women's health and healthcare. 'My history is a shared history', she writes, because '[t]he history of medicine is the history of unwell women, of their bodies, minds and lives'.[9] She is both the author of and participant in the history *Unwell Women* covers, a book – a provocation – driven by argument, expansive in uncovering women's lives that have been neglected, observing that medical ignorance is greater with Black and other women of colour and those at the bottom of the socio-economic ladder, and committed to seeing all these points as part of a complex set of structures. Her work exemplifies entanglement: she writes that recognition of her lupus has meant that, since her diagnosis, she has 'stitched the history of my body, and my life, back together with this new thread of knowledge. I understand, now, that who I have become is indelibly intertwined with my disease'.[10]

The intertwined figure of the sick woman/patient/historian/advocate is a practitioner of an engaged Medical Humanities scholarship, and Cleghorn is one of the indisciplined participants in such academic endeavour. This is not only because of how she weaves her critical modes together, but also because – despite her experiences with an incompetent healthcare system – she is committed to the value of medical science. 'Medicine saved my life', she states bluntly in *Unwell Women*, while she articulates elsewhere an unease with wellness culture because of its potential to overlap with conspiracy theories that deny the need for medical research.[11] Having faith in biomedicine's capacity to make people better and save lines, she makes clear, is not at odds with being a feminist and activist. There is no rejection in her work of any 'medical model' of the body; rather it is models of good medicine that are exactly what's needed. Cleghorn writes in detail about new research that aims to better understand the increase in autoimmune diseases, but also notes that 'we are the most reliable narrators of what is happening in our own bodies'. The science is essential, but, she asserts, 'when a woman tells you that she is in pain, believe her the first time.'[12] There is no need to see the two as incompatible.

There are numerous memoirs from women that describes similar experiences to Cleghorn's. Porochista Khakpour's *Sick* recounts decades spent with undiagnosed Lyme Disease, a condition – like lupus – where insufficient research means that its complex presentation is often misread. And, again like lupus, Lyme is, Khakpour asserts, a condition that affects women more than men, with similar consequences: '[W]omen suffer the most from Lyme', she writes. 'They tend to advance into chronic and late-stage forms of the illness most because often it's checked for last, as doctors often treat them as psychiatric cases first.' She goes on: 'This is why we hear that young women [. . .] are dying of Lyme the fastest. This is also why we hear that chronic illness is a women's burden. Women simply aren't allowed to be sick until they are mentally sick, too, and then it is by some miracle or accident that the two can be separated for proper diagnosis.'[13]

As Khakpour demonstrates, diseases such as Lyme are extraordinarily complex in their expression. Her relapses follow patterns of global, as well as individual, turmoil; geopolitical events that happen on the other side of the world bring on flares, for example. And these slide across associated experiences with PTSD and the various successful and unsuccessful antibiotics that she takes. The result is a continually intertwined and dislocated existence, where the possibility of wholeness always escapes and needs to be reconfigured as a result. 'It has taken many years', she writes, 'to see my own shell, this very body, as a home of sorts. I can report that even now I struggle with this concept, that even as I type these words, something feels outside of myself'. She concludes: 'I sometimes wonder if I would have been less sick if I had had a home.'[14] Home – as a space of recovery and health – is always out of reach and Khakpour's memoir is typical of women's writing about complex misdiagnosis that doesn't presume restitution is possible, even if it might be desired. Like lupus, Lyme is for life, and again like lupus, it is a condition of the inside that creates the feelings of outside Khakpour experiences, a relationship also seen in Cleghorn's struggle with but ultimate acceptance of her lupus as essential to her selfhood.

There are two elements here crucial for my understanding that such perspectives exemplify Medical Humanities critical thinking. The first is that both Khakpour and Cleghorn stress the kind of decentring, especially of the body, increasingly common in Medical Humanities scholarship. Whether concentrating on the patient's body as a focus of healthcare or the very idea of the body's boundaries as a biological, social, and cultural unit, such scholarship sees increasing complexity that destabilizes ingrained humanist concepts of wholeness. The second is that each recounts their body as a site of *writing*. Khakpour's reflection above on the way that she thinks herself into being as she types is matched by Cleghorn's acknowledgment that 'the answers reside in our bodies, and the histories our bodies have always been writing'.[15] Medical Humanities' long tradition of engaging with narratives of lives – a mode of writing Disability Studies often suspects because of its perceived association with individualism and ableist sentimentality – here provides the sophisticated frame that allows for the power of such writing to be better understood.

Bloody women

Endometriosis is a condition around which these questions of bodies, pain, wholeness, home, gender, anger, (mis)diagnosis and treatment cluster to profound effect, and the women who write about it are, like Cleghorn, Khakpour and others, indisciplined proponents of Medical Humanities' ways of critical knowing. As with schizophrenia – and as discussed in the previous chapter – in the abstract endometriosis presents as mysterious, seemingly a puzzle that can only be put together through making mistakes, taking wrong turns or assuming different possibilities. If schizophrenia, the word, signals a terror that looks towards the future, endometriosis often works retrospectively; it is pain, often all-consuming and totalizing, that comes into focus around the word *afterwards*, with the late diagnosis, often after years of suffering. At the same time, both endometriosis and schizophrenia appear to signal an invasion, with the body held hostage by an extraordinary excess, but it is worth noting that the ways that the conditions are seen as 'mysterious' are highly gendered. Where schizophrenia has, in the past, been associated with powerful visions and voices – of the divine, or of grandeur – endometriosis became characterized by its status as a failure of women's bodies and the sexist consequences of this: a threat to young women's progress towards 'natural' pregnancy, for example, or evidence of 'a career-woman's disease'.[16] Over the twentieth century, as schizophrenia appeared to become progressively masculine (especially in conjunction with the 'paranoid' model of male violence) endometriosis emerged as the modern version of the Ancient Greek 'wandering womb', the disruptive and completely gendered source of all female pathologies.

A number of issues exist that make it difficult to be specific about the condition. A major one is uncertainty surrounding its cause. While it's understood that it is the result of cells from within the uterus spreading to other areas of the body, where they then causing the bleeding and scarring that are the source of much of the pain women experience, the exact reason for this is unknown. For much of the twentieth century, the prevailing clinical opinion of endometriosis' origin was a form of 'reverse menstruation' in which menstrual material ('misplaced endometrium') flowed out of the uterus through the fallopian tubes to other parts of the body. It is seen to be, at heart, a disease of the female reproductive system associated with (very) heavy periods and infertility. But there are complications: the lesions found outside of the uterus are not always the same as those found inside and sometimes the structure of these lesions occur in other parts of the body – the lungs, for example – which prompts questions about how the cells that cause the tissue damage get there. In a more clear-cut indicator that the focus on menstruation might be limited, the condition has been found in foetuses. Given that one of the central understandings of endometriosis is that it causes infertility, the fact that pregnant women might have babies with endometrial material seems fundamentally counterintuitive. It also suggests that genetic developments *in utero* may well play a significant part in the condition's origin.[17]

The reason for all these conditionals is that, as with lupus, endometriosis is an under-researched condition and the reason for *this* is because it occurs in women's bodies. Research in all the conditions mentioned in this chapter lags behind those that occur to the same degree in both men and women because complex female embodiment is an outlier in research practice. A consequence of this is that diagnosis and treatment of endometriosis frequently fail to recognize the multiple nature of its presentation. Symptoms can vary, for example, and the fact that the pain involved may fluctuate, displayed in different degrees in different parts of the body across time, is seen as an inconsistency as opposed to an integral part of its manifestation. As a result, the condition is, in Cleghorn's words, 'one of the most frequently misdiagnosed, misunderstood and medically stigmatised chronic diseases', with women having to frequently wait years for the source of their pain to be correctly recognised.[18]

Life writing about endometriosis is often angry. *Endometriosis: It's* NOT *in Your Head, It's in Your Pelvis!* shouts the title of Bethany Stahl's memoir, a sentiment echoed by Gabrielle Jackson's *Pain and Prejudice: A Call to Arms for Women and their Bodies*. Both books are also about collectives: Stahl assures her readers who come to hers because they have the condition that there is a full team of 'endo warriors going through the same situation' who will provide them with support, while Jackson's study is, like Cleghorn's, a combination of personal experience and a history of medical approaches to women's bodies, as well as a response to a major journalistic investigation into endometriosis that involved thousands of women recounting their stories.[19] *Pain and Prejudice* is a sustained polemic, simmering with fury at patriarchal medical practice, failures of diagnosis, structures of control, the limitations of research, government indifference and cultures of victim-blaming. Jackson discusses a range of health conditions but continues to circle back to endometriosis, her own and other's. In 2018, she notes, 'What is endometriosis?' was the third most-Googled question by people searching online for medical information, and Jackson is cautiously optimistic about the raise in the condition's profile and some of the responses to this.[20] But for the most part she continues to believe in the need for the 'call to arms' that is the driving force of her book.

Hilary Mantel and Abby Norman are probably the most well-known figures who write about their experience of endometriosis. As with the direct titles of Stahl and Jackson's books, each invites readers to an active focus on their body: in her memoir *Giving Up the Ghost*, Mantel's chapter on the development of her illness in the 1970s is called 'Show Your Workings', a nice pun on the fact that her pain became chronic during her time as a student; Norman's book, covering the onset of her endometriosis when she was a teenager in the 2010s, is called, straightforwardly, *Ask Me About My Uterus*. Both detail the onset of extreme pain and the ways it spreads out across the body. Mantel writes:

Endometriosis in the intestines makes you vomit and gives you pains in your gut. Pressure in the pelvis makes your back ache, your legs ache. You are too tired to move. The pain, which in the early stages invades you when you menstruate, begins to take over your whole month. Lately I had known days of my life when everything hurt, everything from my collarbone down to my knees.[21]

Added to this was the intense aura that came with migraine headaches, causing confused speech and alterations in visual perception: 'Migraine stirred the air in dull shifts and eddies, charged it with invisible presences and the echoes of strangers' voices; it gave me morbid visions, like visitations, premonitions of dissolution.' At one point, these manifested as a succession of tiny skulls, unrolling, as she puts it, 'like a satanist's wallpaper.'[22]

Norman describes the precise moment she first experienced the condition's full onset:

That's when it happened, and it was as sudden as a thunderclap. A stabbing pain in my middle, as though I were on the receiving end of an unseen assailant's invisible knife [. . .] I pressed a hand against my side, trying to determine exactly where it hurt. It felt like it was everywhere and nowhere all at once. It was almost as though something had snapped deep inside me. I had never experienced anything like it [. . .] The pain became more of an ache, which spread through my lower belly and pelvis, then snaked around my flank toward my back. I began to grow nauseated and dizzy [. . .] My legs were shaking so much I could barely walk.[23]

She goes on to describe the complexities of its presentation:

The struggle to explain what endometriosis actually feels like is very real. The pain itself is of its own breed, yet it feels just similar enough to other pains that when described as such, the possible diagnoses abound. It also exists on a spectrum of severity that means that sometimes the pain level is all-consuming, and other times it's like trying to look at something in your periphery without turning your head. It's there, you know it's there, but it's like trying to catch the air around a bird's wings.[24]

Both writers detail what Mantel refers to as endometriosis' 'dazzling variety of systemic effects'.[25] These are not just chronic pain and exhaustion but also the blame and guilt that Norman identifies as being central to her experience, the feeling that 'deep down in that tangled mess of organs [...] the disease was my fault'.[26] In part, this is a result of the continued misrecognition both women received when seeking medical help, which made each feel – as Cleghorn did – that they must be responsible for their own illness, but also because the condition is bound up with complex processes of individual selfhood and shame. When Norman asks 'Why was I bleeding as though my uterus were a bottomless pool of blood?', she is referencing age-old associations of the female body with disgust, and nearly all accounts of endometriosis make reference to sudden, heavy bleeding and the often traumatic social experiences that result from it. The condition, then, is not only about chronic pain, but the very idea of the female body as a site not only of failure, but punishment; what Mantel, echoing Khakpour, calls the belief 'that the pains which ran through my body each month were part of the burden of womanhood'.[27]

If ever there was a disease enmeshed in entanglement, then, it's endometriosis. The condition makes the body varied and multiple, a site of overlapping expressions and feelings that bring together not only the experiences it produces but the cultures of medical knowledge and healthcare practice that try to identify and treat it. Because of these entanglements, life writing of endometriosis poses challenges for identity-based Disability Studies scholarship. The frequent systemic failure of medical diagnosis and treatment for the condition fits squarely within the classic social model of disability, allowing for critiques of the disabling processes inherent in structures of healthcare and highlighting that the fundamental refusal to believe women when they talk about their own bodies is a characteristic example of an environment driven by an ableist normalcy. But this is only one aspect of experiencing endometriosis, and the interconnections that weave across the individual feeling of pain, the specifics of shame, the spiralling into other illness, and the long cultural history of misrecognition of women's health, create an assemblage of effects that, although profoundly social, exceeds the capacity of such modelling. An advantage of the social model is its portability: because all societies have their own social and cultural determinants of health, each creates structures that perpetuate disabling environments. But the neatness of this argument relies on parameters that cannot deal with the multiplicities and excessiveness of endometrial bodies. This becomes only more true when it's remembered that much disability scholarship still remains suspicious of published life stories, assuming that their trajectories tend towards sentimentality and humanist recovery and restitution. But, to repeat an argument central to this chapter, while the writing of Mantel, Norman, Stahl, Jackson and others shows women may well come to accept endometriosis as a long-term part of their lives, to the extent that it's possible they want to get better. They want better medicine and better treatment that will result in better lives for women in pain.

I haven't read a single word in this writing that assumes that these processes of making better enact a neoliberal expression of the individual and an idea of 'fixing'. Indeed, it is specifically because figures such as Mantel and Norman place their personal experiences within frames that outline histories of discrimination and contemporary sexism that they inevitably dissect humanist concepts of the centred individual and reconstituted wholeness. This dissection is exactly the kind of process explored across the subject areas that make up critical Medical Humanities approaches to the body. New work in the discipline, using models in History, Gender Studies, Cultural Studies and Critical Race Studies among others, has sought to overturn the criticism that in the past Medical Humanities scholarship displayed a functional and pragmatic approach to the body and health, often focused around the authority of the single practitioner (usually male, a point worth stressing here because of the kinds of gendering inherent in treating conditions like endometriosis) and the bounded unit of the single patient. This scholarship addresses precisely the kinds of decentring mentioned above, not only of medical practice – diagnosis, treatment, care and uses of technology, for example – but also the kinds of assumptions about the bodies of women with conditions such as endometriosis. The biological imperative that stresses (in)fertility as the 'most' important element of the condition, for example, can be uncovered to be the often sexist cultural construction of the 'natural' female body that it clearly is (one of Jackson's chapters is titled 'It's the culture, stupid'). Medical Humanities work on embodiment and pain unpicks such suppositions, highlighting social and cultural dimensions of illness alongside the practical elements of pain's 'character', the how as well as the what.[28]

Conclusion: Why do you have to go and make things so complicated?

The critical interrogation this Medical Humanities scholarship practises is shaped by the need to respond to the already-interwoven articulations of health experiences. As their memoirs show, Mantel and Normal experienced other chronic health problems that spiralled out from their original pain. The hallucinations that accompanied Mantel's migraines, as well as doctors' diagnosis of stress following assumptions about her 'overambition', led to her being prescribed anti-depressants and a sequence of events that resulted saw her develop akathisia, a movement disorder characterized by physical restlessness that made it almost impossible for her to remain still. 'The cunning thing about it', Mantel writes in *Giving Up the Ghost*, 'is that it looks, and it feels, exactly like madness. The patient paces. She is unable to stay still. She wears a look of agitation and terror. She wrings her hands; she says she is in hell'.[29] The pain akathisia causes is, Mantel says, actually worse than that of the endometriosis. It is 'the worst thing I have ever experienced, the worst single, defined episode of my entire life':

No physical pain has ever matched that morning's uprush of killing fear, the hammering heart. You are impelled to move, to pace in a small room. You force yourself down into a chair, only to jump out of it. You choke; pressure rises inside your skull. Your hands pull at your clothing and tear at your arms. Your breathing becomes ragged. Your voice is like a bird's cry and your hands flutter like wings. You want to hurl yourself against the windows and walls. Every fibre of your being is possessed by panic.[30]

She continues like this for two more paragraphs, before noting that the response from her doctors to this was to prescribe another anti-psychotic. Injections of Largactil (one of the brand names of Chlorpromazine) removed her madness by crushing her into insensibility and darkness. All of this, because of her misdiagnosed endometriosis.

The conditions associated with Norman's illness related to two specific manifestations. The sheer exhaustion she experienced caused significant weight loss, creating an energy-sapping cycle in which her pain left her often unable to eat, and she was pushed towards a body dysmorphia that was especially triggering because of her mother's bulimia. That family history, in turn, became the source for medical interventions that presumed her illness must be due to psychological trauma that originated in her childhood. Puzzled gynaecologists passed her on to psychoanalysts who read the source of pain in her troubled relationship with her mother. As she went through all these additional appointments, Norman noted: 'I'd want to scream at them that they should have believed me when I said I needed help'.[31] Help, though, was always suggested through modes that paid no attention to what she was saying. 'If I, or any other woman whose gynecological cancers or pathologies had gone undiagnosed, had just been sick in some other part of the body, in some other way, would it have been any different?', she asks. 'Or would it not have mattered? Was the underlying preexisting condition being female?'[32] Going to doctors with pain that emanated in her pelvis and spread throughout her body, with a history of heavy periods and profound, disabling fatigue, Norman was unpicked as a kind of test case for idiopathy. 'You were probably molested as a child and this is just your body's way of dealing with it,' one doctor told her, adding: 'Your problem is complicated [...] Just like *you*.'[33]

I dwell on these examples to show just how far from their uteruses both Mantel and Norman found themselves when they sought medical help and how it became not only easy for them to be designated problems, but seemingly inevitable. That this happened in such similar ways, with so much time between their experiences, drives Norman's anger at the lack of progress in understanding endometriosis. Near the end of *Ask Me About My Uterus*, she makes reference to Mantel's memoir, noting 'Her journey, like mine, began when she was nineteen' and that 'You'd think that in the forty-some years that have elapsed, something would have changed, and a woman my age wouldn't be having the same experience that Mantel [...] had decades ago'.[34] This lineage is the history of mistreating women and failed medical practice, but it's also a kind of haunting, a continuity that's beyond the details of appointments and assessment, even of the pain itself. In Chapter 1 I noted how Meri Nana-Ama Danquah's experience of her depression left her feeling like a ghost and it's intriguing to see that Mantel, Norman and Khakpour all at some point in their books characterize themselves similarly. Mantel's focus on spectres is clear from her memoir's title, and flits across ghosts in houses or the 'something intangible [...] some formless, borderless evil, that came to try to make me despair' that she encounters in a garden when a child.[35] Norman's difficult childhood made her what she calls a 'proficient haunt', someone 'slowly losing my ability to my ability to feel things' because 'no one could apparently see or hear me'.[36] Both writers carried this sense of being an apparition – there and not – through to the embodied experience of their endometriosis. They were present in the consulting rooms and hospitals but also absent, seen but ignored, partly of a ghostly tradition that has included so many women before them.

Khakpour's metaphor is even more complex. She writes of her teenage self:

I felt like a crystal ballerina, a porcelain swan, but most of all like a ghost. The haunting metaphor felt actualized in some part of me: a part-ghost at least. I had access to some other world, but I could be in this one too – I told myself that narrative. The narrative I ignored was the one where I should have also realized that it was the first time I got to feel like a woman – and that perhaps ailment was a feature central to that experience, the lack of wholeness one definition of femaleness, or so they would have you think.[37]

All three women became estranged from their bodies as they began the transition into adulthood and that estrangement was underscored when their illnesses began and their bodies became sites of disbelief. They were ghosted by systems that told them they did not know themselves and then refused explanation. As a result, life was often a nightmare.

In their cultural history of menstruation, Andrew Shail and Gillian Howie observe that across centuries, 'Menstrual discourse has been one of the ways in which the female body has been more intensely described, and the female-embodied described as more bodily, than maleness'.[38] As they note, this has frequently created structures of exclusion through domination, fear and prejudice. But there is another way to think of such intensity. The excessiveness of menstruation is one of those instances where, as many feminist scholars have shown, the body becomes culturally marked through patterns of complexity. All the women discussed in this chapter show how the biological body – bleeding, pained, overflowing, uncontained – is a cultural object, inscribed both in the structures of medicine and through the written modes that seek to articulate experience.[39] Making things complicated in this way is to practice agile, indisciplined volatility, to push back against those versions of health that codify misreadings and perpetuate misunderstanding. Pushing through the pain here is not an example of will or a desire to dominate and reconstitute a centred selfhood, or even necessarily to seek an identity. It is subtler and cleverer than this, producing the need to knit together so many engagements, especially with an ongoing and developing nature of embodiment and its outcomes (particularly pain) and the structured ignorance of medical knowledge and healthcare systems. Mantel, Norman and Khakpour all become creative practitioners in the ways in which they acknowledge and respond to this; their recognition of themselves as ghosts may be negative depictions, but they give language to an experience and together are part of a process that names a world.

As it originated as a discipline, Medical Humanities focused on the power of the clinical moment, whether that be in the consultation room, operating theatre, therapist's office or any other of the many occasions and spaces where such encounters took place. As scholarship in these areas developed in the last ten to twelve years, it became clear that the early concentration on what these moments meant lacks nuance and flexibility. Stories of illness, ideas of personhood, pursuit of practice, institutional policies, measurable outcomes: these and other topics need more than the muted engagement and sometimes-humanist dressing that classic Humanities subject areas can provide. A requirement for new methodologies became obvious as the complexity of the encounters unfurled and Medical Humanities expanded its capacity for critical insight as a consequence. The multiple avenues of enquiry that I have highlighted in this chapter emerged to give sophisticated accounts of what was happening across myriad health effects.

It's a mistake to think that this change is simply another expression of the talent of scholars however, because upon reflection it's clear to see that women who have endometriosis (and others like them) were there first to provide this sophistication. They too sat in spaces where knowledge was limited and clinicians unable to meet the challenge of the people who came to discuss their bodies. And as they then came to voice and write their lives, they went and made it complicated, added the intricacy essential to make meaning of their situation. They argued, provoked and advocated, entangling their pain and experience within the stories of their lives and systems in which they found themselves. They did so through multiple iterations of constant indiscipline; as such they are Medical Humanities insurgents in action and word.

Notes

1. Jean-Dominique Bauby, *The Diving-Bell and the Butterfly* (London: Harper Perennial, 2008), 44 and 25.

2. 'What is MND?', Motor Neurone Disease Association. Available online: https://www.mndassociation.org/about-mnd/what-is-mnd/ (accessed May 24 2022).

3. Public understanding of MND is surely influenced by the life of Stephen Hawking, the most high-profile individual to have had the condition. The fact that Hawking lived for fifty-five years following his initial diagnosis became to be seen as what is possible when someone has MND, as opposed to the truly extraordinary outlier it actually is. That Hawking had a brilliant mind (seemingly trapped inside a body that had ceased to function) only adds to this sense of some kind of potential *capability* within the condition.

4. It is less prevalent now, but Toxic Shock Syndrome (TSS) could easily have been added to this second list. TSS occupies a particular (though not unique)

position in conditions associated with menstruation because of its origins in products, predominantly tampons, and their effect on the body. I learned much about TSS from Sharra L. Vostral's excellent *Toxic Shock: A Social History* (New York: New York University Press, 2018).

5. Bella Bathurst, *Sound: Stories of Hearing Lost and Found* (London: Profile Books, 2017), 202.

6. Felicity Callard, 'Afterword: Mind, Imagination, Affect', *The Edinburgh Companion to the Critical Medical Humanities* (Edinburgh: Edinburgh University Press, 2016), 482.

7. Elinor Cleghorn, *Unwell Women: A Journey Through Medicine and Myth in a Man-Made World* (London: Weidenfeld and Nicolson, 2021), 3.

8. Cleghorn, *Unwell Women*, 406.

9. Ibid., 407. Cleghorn also stresses in her personal biography that, before writing her book, she was a postdoctoral researcher on 'an interdisciplinary medical humanities project' at the University of Oxford. See, for example, her page on her literary agents' website: https://cwagency.co.uk/client/dr-elinor-cleghorn (accessed 7 June 2022).

10. Ibid., 406.

11. Ibid., 409, and Georgia Poplett, 'An interview with Elinor Cleghorn: "History is not a linear road to good"'. Available online: https://lucywritersplatform. com/2022/02/04/an-interview-with-elinor-cleghorn-history-is-not-a-linear-road-to-good/ (accessed 6 June 2022).

12. Cleghorn, *Unwell Women*, 415.

13. Porochista Khakpour, *Sick: A Memoir* (Edinburgh: Canongate, 2018), 166.

14. Khakpour, *Sick*, 168.

15. Cleghorn, *Unwell Women*, 19.

16. Ibid., 306–11.

17. Pietro Signorile et al., 'New Evidence of the Presence of Endometriosis in the Human Fetus', *Reproductive BioMedicine Online* 21, no. 1 (2010): 142–7. Available online: https://www.rbmojournal.com/article/S1472-6483(10)00179-3/fulltext (accessed 13 June 2022).

18. Cleghorn, *Unwell Women*, 310.

19. Bethany Stahl, *Endometriosis: It's NOT in Your Head, It's in Your Pelvis* (Privately published, 2019), 1. Gabrielle Jackson, *Pain and Prejudice: A Call to Arms for Women and their Bodies* (London: Piatkus, 2019). Jackson first wrote about her condition for *The Guardian* in 2015, an article that prompted the paper to undertake a major global investigation of women's experience of the condition: 'I'm not a hypochondriac. I have a disease. All these things that are wrong with me are real, they are endometriosis.' Available online. https://www.theguardian.com/society/2015/sep/28/im-not-a-hypochondriac-i-have-a-disease-all-these-things-that-are-wrong-with-me-are-real-they-are-endometriosis (accessed 14 June 2022).

20. Jackson, *Pain and Prejudice*, 315.

21. Hilary Mantel, *Giving Up the Ghost: A Memoir* (London: Fourth Estate, 2013), 192. I'm grateful to Neko Mellor for helping me understand endometriosis, especially in relation to Mantel and Norman's writing.

22. Mantel, *Giving Up the Ghost*, 193.

23. Abby Norman, *Ask Me About My Uterus: A Quest to Make Doctors Believe in Women's Pain* (New York: Bold Type Books, 2019), 2–3.

24. Norman, *Ask Me About My Uterus*, 51.

25. Mantel, *Giving Up the Ghost*, 190.

26. Norman, *Ask Me About My Uterus*, 46.

27. Mantel, *Giving Up the Ghost*, 209.

28. See, for example, Suzannah Biernoff's essay 'Picturing Pain' in *The Edinburgh Companion to the Medical Humanities*, 163–85. Biernoff's focus on images of pain stresses not simply the idea of a 'picture "of" pain' but also 'ways of performing or "doing" pain', where the idea of 'doing' is informed by precisely the kind of amalgamation of history, gender studies, aesthetic theory, and movement beyond narrative that is typical of Medical Humanities research.

29. Mantel, *Giving Up the Ghost*, 181.

30. Ibid., 181–2.

31. Norman, *Ask Me About My Uterus*, 90.

32. Ibid., 23.

33. Ibid. 128.

34. Ibid., 187.

35. Mantel, *Giving Up the Ghost*, 107. The final chapter of Mantel's book is called 'Afterlife'.

36. Norman, *Ask Me About My Uterus*, 70.

37. Khakpour, *Sick*, 36.

38. Andrew Shail and Gillian Howie, 'Introduction: "Talking Your Body's Language": The Menstrual Materialisations of Sexed Ontology', in *Menstruation: A Cultural History*, ed. Shail and Howie, (Basingstoke: Palgrave Macmillan, 2005), 3.

39. Probably the foundational critical figure most associated with this is Elizabeth Grosz, especially in *Volatile Bodies: Towards a Corporeal Feminism* (Bloomington: Indiana University Press: 1994).

REFLECTION 4: OUTSIDE THE FRAME

I am travelling to see my sister Alison, a long train journey from the North to the South of England that takes nearly five hours. Alison was diagnosed with Motor Neurone Disease as I first began this book and my encounter with her experience has shaped much of its contents in different ways. As her condition has worsened, I've done more of these trips and more reading and writing in the bubble created by the travel. Before leaving, I had asked her on a WhatsApp call if there was anything in particular she wanted me to bring down. MND has taught me the precision of such a question: it is not simply asking about a luxury or something that might make her happy; it is the practicality of something she might need to have within reach, something essential as her mobility decreases and others struggled to understand her. 'Cards,' she says, and pauses, wiping her mouth from the build-up of saliva caused by the difficulties she has swallowing. 'Flash cards,' each word said precisely in a way that signals her knowledge and frustration with how she speaks. Her reply confuses me and I wonder if I've misheard. 'Flash cards so I can let people know what I need.' She tells me that her speech is at its worst first thing in the morning and when staff at the care home at which she lives come to her room, she has difficulty explaining where she keeps the objects – medicine, cups, cushions, clothes – that she needs to start the day. Often day staff will have had little or no contact with the night staff they are replacing, meaning there is no continuity in the passing on of information. Something that happened in the night will not have been communicated to the new arrivals and the sheer labour of trying to explain it again is both exhausting and, increasingly, becoming impossible. In addition, many of the workers at her home are agency staff and not all have English as their first language. Alison tells me that this adds to the problems.

Right, flash cards then. What does she want written on them? 'Tea,' 'Coffee,' she says. 'Water.' I'm trying to be positive but this last horrifies me and for a few seconds I can't say anything. To need a card to ask for one of the most basic things in life. Unconnected, Alison laughs. 'And under the bed,' she adds, stopping to wipe her mouth again. 'Under the bed?', I repeat. 'Yes' – she positively trills this, loving the absurdity. 'A lot of what I need is under my bed! They put things there and forget them and then when I need it I can't tell them or point. If I can say it's under the bed, they'll know where to look.'

As her energy levels drop, speech becomes more difficult, so we finish. I feel completely thrown. It never occurred to me that something like this might be necessary. Alison had been part of a Google trial to record words and phrases that could be adapted for assisted communication software for people with MND. We'd taken the project seriously, recording all sorts of things that might help in the future, but it also presented so many opportunities to play and joke: we support rival football teams and I found endless delight in making her tablet announce that mine was vastly superior to hers – all at the touch of a button. As her condition progressed, however, talking about the technology had fallen away and stopped feeling relevant when the realities of care became more basic.

I'm carrying the cards on the train. My children have drawn and coloured them: a clear glass of water; a mug of coffee and cup of tea, each with hot, steaming lines coming out of the top; and a line drawing of a bed, side on and with a large coloured arrow pointing underneath. Each has the relevant words clearly spelled out. Something else is on my mind, however. 'Like Lucas had,' Alison had said when we spoke – saying it twice because the 'Lu' had been difficult to get out. 'Like Lucas had'. When he was a young child and it was clear that his speech was not going to develop, and before the days of programmable software, Lucas had used a Picture Exchange Communication System, or PECS. PECS consisted of a series of small cards with line-drawn images, symbols or words – 'bed', 'toilet', 'first ... then ...', 'I want', 'No' – attached by Velcro to a book-like folder that included a sentence strip across the bottom. The idea was that he would take separate cards and arrange them into sentences, the beginning of a communicative language. It never happened. Why say 'I want crisps' when you can just grab the 'crisps' symbol? And why put it on the strip when you can just hand it to any nearby adult? I knew the logic and tried to follow the rules, but basically admired how he short-circuited the system and made it work for him (plus, if you know which cupboard the crisps are in, why bother asking at all?). Over time, the cards were lost – under the fridge, behind the sofa, outdoors. The iPad software I describe in the second memory vignette of this book is basically the same though, and longer lasting.

But for PECS – because that's what it was – to come back now ... Not 'crisps' for an autistic boy, but 'water' for an adult losing her speech. I'm attuned to a lot of the difficulties that come with certain disabilities; more often than not they just have to be met because they're practicalities and need doing first and thinking about later, but this affects me. PECS had been a bad place, a process that in the end was futile, part of what felt like a downward spiral that seemingly had no end. As the train ran south, I tried not to think of continuity, of experiences come full circle. I knew that's not what it was – the circumstances were so different – but it was an impossible feeling to shake.

Alison's care home is chaotic and largely dysfunctional, a product of a privatized healthcare system that seems to have accepted its creation of incompetence and indifference hidden behind slogans, one that signals good intentions but knows it doesn't deliver them and often seems not to care. I was amazed when she first told me that she knew before the move that it would be like this – 'this crap,' she says with a laugh. What did I expect? Genuine care? Whole books are written about care – philosophical, social, touch and affect, interdependence, assistive technologies – and in attempting to engage with Alison's experience with hindsight, I can see it's deeply structural in ways these studies suggest. But this knowledge is elsewhere as I try to deal with this one specific – grounded, located – example of her home. My sister is a troublemaker, asking questions about lack of consultation or cleanliness, but she is always aware to keep the right side of a line. In the end the people she talks to have extraordinary power over her, a power that will only extend over the coming months. But in a home largely full of older adults with Alzheimer's and other forms of dementia, who she feels might not be able to express themselves on these issues as much as she can, she is – for now – articulate and opinionated, often demanding to speak to the home's management.

One of the many current problems is that staff on the two floors of the building aren't speaking to one another. The cost of living in the home is considerable, but the bulk of the staff (which includes permanent employees and agency workers) are paid basic wages. Some care and work more than others and resentment builds across the different workspaces. It's understood that this is the fault of the management, because of the poor pay, but the fall-out is felt by those – both staff and residents – who live with the day-to-day consequences. I'm learning just how much everything about any end-of-life condition is inevitably about configurations of care. Health is a network here, a spiral, a vortex. When I visit, I have to negotiate whichever dynamic is at work on any given day: finding where to empty a bin; chasing late medication; tracking down a lost cushion.

Seeing Alison each visit is to see her body consistently change. It's increasingly difficult for her to hold her head up, and many of our recent conversations have revolved around which neck-support product might be the best one to choose to help with this. Her hands move less and are more painful, and each time she is slightly more curved in on herself, slightly further to one side, and her legs are thinner. For months now she has been unable to eat because of her difficulties swallowing and she feeds herself through a tube. I try to put this view of her body within the context of how I have seen it in the past, but realize this is belated. I can't remember what I have thought about her body before, so to try now would be to reconstruct it. I know that this is inevitable but still feel it to be knowledge I want to have. I wrote much of the preceding chapter on endometriosis and women's bodies as my travels to see Alison became more frequent and although the contexts are different, MND is equally about embodiment. As I see her now I think of this.

Recently, at home, we rediscovered a collection of slides from the 1970s; blue and white, or yellow, squares, cardboard and plastic, with Kodak printed on some, framing tiny family photographs across various holidays. We selected the best of these, scanned them, and collected them into a photobook that I took down to Alison on one of my visits. In one, taken in the mid-1970s, I'm standing with her and our father under a tree on a beach. Alison is around fourteen or fifteen and wearing a bikini. She's standing at an angle to the camera with both arms raised to, lightly, put her weight on a branch and there's a slight bend in the leg closest to the lens, the hint maybe of a pose. Her body is tanned, loose and relaxed, healthy and anticipating womanhood. Our mother is probably not in the photo because, although tall and elegant, she was always deeply uncomfortable when having her picture taken, self-conscious about her body. One mechanism she developed to deal with this was to point out of the frame when the camera was on her, to make the image meaningful by it somehow not being about her, but rather rendering her body an action, a literal signpost to something else, something that can't be seen. For all that this is evidently so self-conscious, I imagine that it made it easier to be singled out if you can somehow deflect the gaze.

In another photograph, my sister is doing the same. Almost certainly prompted by our mother, she is side on to the camera, pointing off to the right. She is leaning back slightly as if her body is facing into a wind, and laughing. Maybe because she is impersonating? Maybe it's the irony of knowing that she is in fact happy to be in the picture but enacting the embodiment of someone who isn't. Maybe because there is actually something to point at? A nice private joke. I think of this as I see her hands now, as we discuss where to put the flash cards and how they will be within reach. 'Are you going to hold them or point to them?', I ask. She laughs at my stupid pedantry. 'Depends, doesn't it?', she replies, stopping to again wipe her mouth. 'Depends what I can do.'

As a disease, MND is never missing, though it can be missed. When it arrives, it is often hidden and discovered only when other possible causes – muscular, neurological – have been looked for and discounted (in this, it shares some similarities with endometriosis). When found, it is acknowledged as the last word. It gathers pace and misses nothing. It is progressive and pervasive, totally structural, remorseless and uninterested in ambiguity. Seen on its own terms, it has no time whatsoever for – indeed scorns the very idea of – the complex interweavings that I've tried to claim typify disability and health experiences in this book. In fact, it's senseless even to characterize it in this way, to suggest it somehow has decision-making powers. That's not at all how it works. Often I feel that my thinking and writing get over-relativistic, and when this happens I can find myself arguing that health manifests as both everything and nothing, presence and absence, in full view and hiding. But MND is incrementally and endlessly everything, immune to intervention or argument. Like some other conditions, it takes the provisional away from the future and replaces it with certainty. It might play with time and have diversions, but on its own terms it is brutally linear. I understand that I'm characterizing it again, but it doesn't care.

If I couldn't remember what I thought of Alison's body before MND arrived, I can see it in the pictures. As we sit in her room and turn the pages of the photobook, seeing our younger selves, she fills me in on the family stories she knows I don't know (she is nine years older than me). This is an intimate moment, quiet and poignant; we have no other siblings and are aware that if she doesn't do this now, then the knowledge will be lost forever. It is a combination of the trivial (which beach we're on in one of the photos) and the profound (I didn't know the full details of our mother's psychosis, mentioned at the end of the previous chapter, until one of these conversations) and is accompanied by the mix of the her body now – the difficulties holding her head up, the pauses to wipe her mouth – and then, the teenager posing, laughing and pointing.

I realize that I like the pointing especially, because it's her body indicating the so-much-more that all bodies encounter, one way or another. I know that my mother's pointing was forced, maybe even desperate, and that ill health dominated much of her life, and I know that my sister's body is disabling her further every day. But here it is, suggestive of all sorts of things: the journey *from then to now, maybe; from health to disability but also from childhood to adulthood; from her to me. Yep, look – out there.*

Alison died a month after I completed the manuscript for this book. By coincidence, at her funeral her daughters chose the first photograph I describe here to be part of the slideshow portraying her life on a big screen as her coffin entered the chapel.

CONCLUSION: AGILE

In the spring of 2022, two events took place that brought specific instances of health and disability into high-profile focus. In March, at the Academy Awards in Los Angeles, actor Will Smith struck comedian and host Chris Rock in response to a joke Rock made about Smith's wife, actor Jada Pinkett Smith, who has alopecia. When she shaved her head in 2021, Pinkett Smith made it clear that she was acting in a direct response to the condition, posting images of herself on Instagram and declaring 'Me and this alopecia are going to be friends . . . period!'. Smith's actions totally overshadowed the rest of the awards ceremony and created a firestorm of debate about the rights and wrongs of the situation, as well as providing a sudden focus on alopecia itself. Three days later, and less explosively, the family of actor Bruce Willis announced that he would no longer be making films as a result of a recent diagnosis of aphasia. Willis's family statement noted that the condition had affected his cognitive abilities to a point where he was unable to carry on with his career.

Much was said about both events, but one point they had in common was a discussion of exactly how alopecia and aphasia are disabilities. Willis's news was greeted with a slew of 'What is aphasia?' news pieces ('Never heard of aphasia? You're not alone') that explained the causes, forms and consequences of the condition and expressed near-universal sympathy for the actor.[1] Pinkett Smith's situation was far more complicated. Her alopecia became bound in a set of other questions that were prompted by the events of the awards ceremony, particularly Rock's decision to base a joke around her appearance and Smith's violence as a response. Central to this was whether Rock – who had already delivered a series of jokes about the looks of other members of the event's audience – crossed a boundary by specifically identifying Pinkett Smith's alopecia. You can be the subject of a joke because you're ugly, Rock's logic seemed to run, or because you're old, so why not because your hair was falling out and you decided to shave your head. And what exactly constitutes humour in such a situation? Rock has built a career on being 'direct' and inflammatory; he's happy to be cruel. Is there a difference between such a technique when directed at someone with a disability as opposed to someone with physical characteristics that are not understood as disabling? If so, how can that difference be articulated? It appeared that most people in the audience laughed at the joke and later there was much more condemnation for Smith's actions than for Rock's words.[2]

In their different ways, both Pinkett Smith and Willis generated one of those once-in-a-while highly public conversation about what disability means. In Willis's case, the case was complex but apparently explainable. Neurology, language loss, and ageing arguably receive greater public awareness than ever before and people know of their complications, even if they don't know the precise ways in which they manifest or the terms used to describe them. But, again, Pinkett Smith is different. Alopecia is an autoimmune condition and incurable, although hair can regrow as the follicles themselves are rarely attacked. As with many other autoimmune conditions, though, it presents as a kind of mistake, the body inexplicably turning on itself. And mistakes in the body, while common, are often hard to understand. Ageing is the body in predictable decline; autoimmune conditions are the body going *wrong*. In addition, because Pinkett Smith's disability is so visual it seemed especially confusing. Encounters with alopecia are visceral events that seem to make staring – that most fundamental of disability reactions – inevitable, particularly because people with the condition are often assumed to be having chemotherapy treatment for cancer.

And, of course and always, gender and culture matter. Willis's film language was marked by a certain eloquence, with memorable one-liners associated with the kind of white masculinity he projected, and more generally an actor being unable to speak is a *recognizable* problem. Pinkett Smith is a Black woman working in a world where appearance is at a premium and judgment passed on a daily basis. Hair is a statement, as can be the decision not to have it. The inherent sexism that was part of the sudden focus on Pinkett Smith saw her disability viewed as somehow being illegitimate because of this, that her shaved head might be an affectation given its connection to presentation, a lifestyle choice in some way. In addition, Willis's aphasia seems understandably *disabling*, taking away a core function of human expression. Pinkett Smith just had less hair, something that in the days that followed seemed for many to be more of an inconvenience than an actual disability. Interestingly, but in very different ways, both central figures were silent as their stories unfurled: Willis's family spoke for him (an act given power as his condition focuses on problems with speech); while Pinkett Smith was spoken about by Rock, and then 'defended' by Smith. While Pinkett Smith could be seen – indeed in close-up, sitting at the ceremony while events unfolded – it was arguably her silence, while others determined how she might feel, or what she meant, that was the strongest example not only of her position as a woman, but of her being disabled.

The two examples demonstrate the sliding scales of disability and health experiences. At the risk of stating the obvious, complexity is everything, and the Pinkett Smith and Willis narratives are highly complex, mixing the experience and manifestation of disability and health conditions with intricacies of public perception and social/cultural dynamics. I have probably overused the word 'complex' in this book, largely because of a split dynamic. I'm aware that most of the topics on which I've focused haven't been covered in enough complexity because of the constraints of space, but also I know that I've always been pushing towards the greatest complexity I can find in the examples I do use in order to try and do them justice.

I've thought about the kind of scholarship that can enact such justice. What do those of us who work in Medical Humanities and Disability Studies want to practise in order to address the subjects on which we work? As I have said across the previous chapters, the idea and term I have found myself coming back to as I came towards finishing this book is agility. By this I mean an agile scholarship that can be receptive and aware, move across topics and within detail, and not be confined within and intimidated by disciplinary boundaries. At the same time, it can still feel insecure, anxious of its location and even pursued by detractors as it undertakes its work.[3] I think it's undoubtedly provocative to call for agility in contexts of health and disability, because it can arguably be ableist to focus on movement in this way. Agility suggests mobility and flexibility, terms that so frequently work against 'unhealthy' and disabled bodies (in basic issues of accessibility, for example, with the presumption about what bodies 'can do' when they encounter non-disabled environments, be these literal or more widely ideological). 'Upward mobility' is an especially cruel term when read through a disability lens, combining a metaphor of motion with ides of career development and the kinds of advancement denied to many disabled people.

But agility is other things. It can be versatility, cunning, escape, intelligence, opposition. (It's an irony that the specific barb in Rock's comments to Pinkett Smith, that her shaved head meant she could star as the titular character in any remake of the 1997 feature *G.I. Jane*, missed the fact that Demi Moore's performance in the film is full of constant agility.)[4] I value these terms because I have found them across the incredible material I have read and heard putting this book together. And it's important to stress that they are not only words applied from without to describe experience: they are *derived from* disability and health equally. Disability agility is everywhere. Members of disability dance, circus and theatre companies are fabulously, creatively agile; disabled athletes are powerfully agile; Deaf signing is brilliantly agile; an autistic child playing with a slinky is agile, creating patterns that would defeat many others who attempt to copy them.

Health agility might seem more difficult to name – health systems are, after all, notoriously and problematically inflexible – but maybe its ordinary manifestations are no less valuable: rehabilitation, physiotherapy, increasing mobility during ageing. These overlap with disability of course and for all that they might lack drama can be seen as the everyday counterparts to the spectacular nature of disabled dance and sport. Rehabilitation may be a loaded term for some, in its suggestion of making a body better because of suppositions about what that body is supposed to be. But if rehabilitation helps a disabled person to lead the life they want, I can't see that as a problem. As all health and disability stories attest, language matters and metaphors can be problematic, but that doesn't mean they create an unbreakable hold on how those stories can be expressed.

And agility can also be humility. Specifically because it's not entrenched, it can accept the need to pause and doubt, to think about the next move, to plan carefully, sensitivity, ethically. The ways that Medical Humanities scholarship works across subjects, trying to build complexity, can be seen as a desire for an intellectual agility in this humble way. Similarly, agility be a word and idea that Disability Studies can claim as, recognizing the need for a humility in its approaches, it asserts the worth of people and disabled lives. In doing this, agility can also be communal, because it is a set of meeting spaces for scholars, practitioners and activists These ideas are not revolutionary maybe, and are practised in other critical moments (I think of the movement suggested in the Deluezian concept of 'becoming', for example, a central reference point in critical posthumanist theory) but we might better know Jada Pinkett Smith's situation, and that of others like her, if we can commit to a positive agility – a hoped-for humble and communal energy – in our thinking, reading, writing and practice.

The life stories that have dominated this book speak time and again of the power of agility and versatility and it's finding the ideas in these sources that in the end is most inspiring for me. To return to one of the texts that was foundational to my thinking: in Jan Grue's *I Live a Live Like Yours*, there is a wonderful scene in which Grue recounts a childhood experience of attending a friend's birthday party and skating in his wheelchair on an ice-covered field in a playground:

I figure out that I can use my wheelchair as a sled. I start by driving very fast, slam on the brakes, and off I go, gliding across the ice, spinning around once, twice, three times. It's entirely friction-free, and then it turns magical. Someone hitches onto the wheelchair, grabs the basket behind the seat. I continue driving, pulling them along. A tail of children cobbles onto the wheelchair, grows longer. They are drawn to me from around the courtyard, like iron filings to a magnet.[5]

Ten years later, Grue sees the 1933 film *Footlight Parade*, famous for its dance scenes choreographed by the legendary Busby Berkeley. As he watches its perfect synchronization, he says: 'It takes me a while to understand what I am seeing, what I remember.' And the memory of the party the film sparks reminds him that it was the first time he realized that 'it was possible to move without thinking about *how* I moved, without fear of falling'.[6] As he skates, Grue becomes a point of focus, drawing children to him to enact patterns that cannot be replicated without a wheelchair. The dance is a fabulous assertion of Grue's disabled selfhood, the beauty of his agility that of a classic Hollywood musical.

I am claiming that a dance such as Grue's is an example of indiscipline, a specific kind of breaking of norms that exemplifies the ideas I've tried to outline across this book's arguments. It is a product of an agile energy that can be transferred to scholarship (it's a shame that scholars can't really do magic, but we can possibly find it in our sources, as here). Such an energy might allow a commitment to thought and practice that understands the value of working within disciplines and subject areas, but does so through models that disrupt and problematize – crip, queer, complain, assert, challenge, miss, doubt, unveil, synthesize, create – what health and disability mean. And this can be done in tandem and more; there is no requirement that one discipline somehow needs more to correct the other, no moral high ground.

In my Introduction, I observed that I'm wary of critical writing that claims a *need* for scholarship to operate in a certain way, so it would be hypocritical of me to make such a claim now. Clearly what I have said about indiscipline isn't the only way to conceive the relationship between the disciplines that are the focus of this book and, as the poem that follows this Conclusion shows, there is inevitably more to be said about health and its consequences and registers for that saying will change. I also said in the Introduction, however, that thinking about the relationship was an exercise in letting it suggest to me how such a conception might be undertaken and I have followed this through as my reading and writing developed. Throughout, I have leaned on the fact that my approach is designed to be a provocation and this has been a vital guide. A critical provocation has to choose a path, one that emerges as material comes together and suggests directions. Saying I followed such a path is true, but I shouldn't suggest that my own movements have somehow been passive, that I'm only a follower. Placing a dictionary definition of provocation at the start was an intended statement, an admission that the book is a kind of test that aims to produce a response, so I own that position as well. If the result is in/, un/, or even ill/disciplined, if – like Grue's dance – it turns out to be unexpected, then it's done its job.

Notes

1. Abby Foster and Caroline Baker, 'What is aphasia, the condition Bruce Willis lives with?'. Available online: https://theconversation.com/what-is-aphasia-the-condition-bruce-willis-lives-with-180399 (accessed 18 April 2022).

2. In the midst of the consternation, the irony that the Award for Best Picture went to *CODA*, a melodrama about family and deafness, went largely unstated.

3. In thinking about agile scholarship, I'm grateful to all the participants who discussed the topic at a workshop on Affective Technotouch held at the Brocher Foundation in Geneva in June 2022, especially event organizers Amelia DeFalco and Luna Dolezal.

4. I should stress that in making this point, I'm not trying to reclaim the film as being progressive in any way. After the Academy Awards furore, I realized that I had never seen *G.I. Jane*, so watched it. It's a terrible film in which Moore's character goes through gruelling military training, complete with predictable brutality and misogyny, in order to emerge triumphant at the story's close in a mission to retrieve some plutonium lost in the Libyan desert. It's a not-remotely-veiled piece of rampant voyeuristic, sexist, colonial propaganda, marked by an appalling script and uniformly awful acting. And all in the name of supposed feminism. In one scene of sustained graphic violence, Moore is tied to a chair with her hands behind her back and beaten/tortured by a senior officer, including being held underwater. Predictably, she fights back and, even while constrained, 'proves' herself through matching violence with violence. And she does so with great agility, physically outmanoeuvring her assailant on numerous occasions. While the scene is not enough to redeem the film, I like to imagine it as a retort Pinkett Smith might have made to Rock; that her version of *G.I. Jane* would have reduced him to a broken, battered figure lying in the dust. I really can't imagine that anyone is ever going to make a sequel, however.

5. Jan Grue, *I Live a Life Like Yours* (London: Pushkin Press, 2021), 89.

6. Grue, *I Live a Life Like Yours*, 90 and 91. Italics in original.

LAST

Imagine a train ... delayed ... delayed ... delayed'

Leontia Flynn

As we arrived after the staff's call, you stood at the end of your bed.
Slacks neatly creased, V-necked jumper, shirt, tie half-Windsored,
Your shoes shined by fluttering hands
With rings worn from a lifetime moved up one finger;
Your watch swinging from a lighter wrist,
A single link carefully removed.
Outside, the streets sound of autumn's leaving,
Thinning trees of darker orange closer still.

Once again, you had packed your bag.
It would be all right, you knew.
You would get the train to the other station,
With its ticket booths and posters of
Primary-coloured days away.
Taxi from there to the hotel,
Marked as summer, where you still smooth your black hair back,
A widow's peak pointing like a sign to a return of tall holiday nights,
Calendar years of beach throw and catch.

So, it will take time to persuade you that you can't:
Can't remember the intolerant distances,
Rapids of time, late littering harvests;
Or the words that sit in the clotted air, just said
But already misplaced, suspicious.
Can't ask, or expect answers,
Can't go, can't get back.

Stood in your room,
The door will open once only,

And the scrubbed fields of days tilt back to where your adulthood began:
A wardrobe, chair,
Brown bag packed at the end of a neatly made bed;
Nervous goodbye, not knowing what comes next beyond travel,
Already raging at what others won't remember.

INDEX

Index

Index